FPQP Exam

Practice Question Workbook

ISBN: 1957426918
ISBN-13: 978-1957426914

CONTENTS

PRACTICE EXAM 1

QUESTIONS

1. **All but which of the following are characteristics of a sole proprietorship?**

   A. It's the simplest form of business entity.
   B. It has no formal legal requirements.
   C. It has a lack of continuity of business life.
   D. It provides limited liability for the owner.

2. **A car loan payment would appear on which of the following financial statements?**

   A. Statement of financial position
   B. Cash flow statement
   C. Income statement
   D. None of the above are correct.

3. **Which of the following is a type of beneficiary designation in which the policyholder does not retain the right to change the beneficiary without restriction?**

   A. Irrevocable
   B. Revocable
   C. Primary
   D. Contingent

4. **All but which of the following are correct regarding a will codicil?**

   A. If a testator is legally competent, he or she may execute a codicil.
   B. A codicil is suitable for a minor will revision such as changing a specific bequest.
   C. A codicil may be used to update a beneficiary's legal name due to marriage or divorce.
   D. All of the above are correct.

5. **Which of the following is correct regarding the impact that a high estimated inflation rate has on achieving a financial goal?**

   A. It will require allocating fewer dollars toward achieving the goal.
   B. It will require allocating more dollars toward achieving the goal.
   C. It will require allocating the same amount of dollars toward achieving the goal that a low estimated inflation rate would require.
   D. The estimated inflation rate will have no effect on allocating dollars toward achieving the goal.

6. **Which of the following is correct regarding vesting for a SEP IRA?**

   A. Either cliff vesting or graded vesting is allowed for contributions.
   B. Contributions may take up to 3 years to vest.
   C. Contributions may take up to 6 years to vest.
   D. Contributions vest immediately.

7. Which of the following is a written document that provides all material information about an offering of securities and is the primary sales tool of the company that issues the securities?

A. Form 10-K
B. Indenture
C. Prospectus
D. IPO

8. All but which of the following are types of partnerships?

A. Estate partnership
B. General partnership
C. Limited partnership
D. Limited liability partnership

9. Which of the following describes any retirement plan that meets the applicable requirements of the Internal Revenue Code for tax-favored treatment?

A. Nonqualified plan
B. Qualified plan
C. Defined contribution plan
D. Defined benefit plan

10. All but which of the following may be accomplished through a testamentary trust?

A. Avoid probate.
B. Reduce estate taxes.
C. Provide professional investment management.
D. Ensure property in a decedent's estate is passed according to the decedent's wishes.

11. Which of the following steps of the financial planning process comes directly after understanding the client's personal and financial circumstances?

A. Analyzing the client's current course of action and potential alternate courses of action.
B. Presenting the financial planning recommendations.
C. Identifying and selecting goals.
D. Developing the financial planning recommendations.

12. Which of the following is correct regarding TIPS?

A. Interest earned from TIPS may be excluded from income if proceeds are used to pay for qualified higher education expenses.
B. The principal of TIPS increases with inflation and decreases with deflation.
C. TIPS are issued by corporations with high credit ratings.
D. None of the above are correct.

13. Which of the following parts of a personal automobile policy (PAP) are paired with the correct description?

(1) Part A: Liability coverage
(2) Part E: General provisions
(3) Part C: Uninsured motorist coverage
(4) Part F: Duties after an accident or loss

A. (1) and (3) only
B. (2) and (4) only
C. None of the above are correct.
D. All of the above are correct.

14. Employer contributions to a defined contribution plan must use either the ______ cliff vesting or ______ graded vesting schedules.

A. 3-year; 6-year
B. 3-year; 7-year
C. 5-year; 6-year
D. 5-year; 7-year

15. Which of the following represent highly regarded, well-established companies that have demonstrated the ability to operate profitably in both positive and negative economic climates?

A. Sector stocks
B. Common stocks
C. Preferred stocks
D. Blue chip stocks

16. Which of the following is the percentage of taxable income that an individual pays in taxes?

A. Gross tax rate
B. Marginal tax rate
C. Effective tax rate
D. Progressive tax rate

17. Which of the following debts may be discharged through bankruptcy court?

(1) Car loans
(2) Alimony
(3) Government loans
(4) Child support
(5) Credit card debt

A. (1) and (5) only
B. (2) and (4) only
C. (1), (2), and (5) only
D. (2), (3), and (4) only

18. Which of the following is a type of joint ownership of real property in which ownership is split between a present interest and a remainder interest?

A. Gross estate
B. Life estate
C. Joint estate
D. Grantor estate

19. Which of the following describes the relationship between total risk, systematic risk, and unsystematic risk?

A. Total risk = systematic risk – unsystematic risk
B. Total risk – systematic risk = unsystematic risk
C. Unsystematic risk – total risk = systematic risk
D. Total risk + unsystematic risk = systematic risk

20. Which of the following is a type of permanent life insurance in which the cash value and death benefit vary according to the value of underlying investments selected by the insured?

A. Universal life insurance
B. Term life insurance
C. Variable life insurance
D. None of the above are correct.

21. COBRA continuation coverage is provided to which of the following employees?

(1) Employees who are voluntarily terminated for gross misconduct.
(2) Employees who are voluntarily terminated for reasons except gross misconduct.
(3) Employees who are involuntarily terminated for gross misconduct.
(4) Employees who are involuntarily terminated for reasons except gross misconduct.

A. (2) only
B. (2) and (4) only
C. (1), (2), and (4) only
D. All of the above are correct.

22. An individual who creates a last will and testament is known as a:

A. grantor.
B. trustor.
C. settlor.
D. testator.

23. Relating to the time value of money, which of the following is a payment that increases each period to keep up with inflation?

A. Standard payment
B. Adjusted payment
C. Serial payment
D. Present value payment

24. Which of the following is correct regarding the conversion provision in a life insurance policy?

A. The insured may convert from term life insurance to long-term care insurance without having to show evidence of insurability.
B. The insured may convert from permanent life insurance to disability insurance without having to show evidence of insurability.
C. The insured may convert from term life insurance to disability insurance without having to show evidence of insurability.
D. The insured may convert from term life insurance to permanent life insurance without having to show evidence of insurability.

25. A stock with a beta of −1.2 will change in which of the following ways if the stock market increases by 4%?

A. Increase by 2.8%.
B. Increase by 4.8%.
C. Decrease by 4.8%.
D. Decrease by 5.4%.

26. Which of the following is a needs-based social welfare program that provides benefits to low-income adults, their families, and individuals with certain disabilities?

A. Medicaid
B. Medicare
C. Medigap
D. COBRA

27. Which of the following are among the exemptions from the 10% early withdrawal penalty from an IRA?

(1) Hardship withdrawals
(2) Higher education expenses for the account owner's child
(3) First-time home purchase up to $10,000
(4) Loan for qualified education expenses

A. (1) and (4) only
B. (2) and (3) only
C. (1), (2), and (3) only
D. All of the above are correct.

28. Which of the following Acts protects consumers against inaccurate and unfair credit card practices and requires lenders to provide loan cost information so that consumers can comparison shop for certain types of loans?

A. Fair and Accurate Credit Transactions Act (FACTA)
B. Truth in Lending Act (TILA)
C. Equal Credit Opportunity Act (ECOA)
D. Fair Debt Collection Practices Act (FDCPA)

29. If an investor uses dollar cost averaging, ______ shares of an investment will be purchased when the share price is low and ______ shares when the share price is high.

A. more; fewer
B. fewer; more
C. more; more
D. fewer; fewer

30. All but which of the following are considered community property?

A. Property acquired by either spouse prior to marriage.
B. Property acquired by either spouse during marriage by gift.
C. Property acquired by either spouse during marriage by inheritance.
D. None of the above are correct.

31. Which of the following are types of buy-sell agreements?

(1) Cross-purchase agreement
(2) Entity-purchase agreement
(3) Cross-entity agreement
(4) Entity-unit agreement

A. (1) and (2) only
B. (1) and (3) only
C. (2) and (3) only
D. (3) and (4) only

32. Equity income mutual funds generally invest in stocks that pay:

A. no dividends.
B. above average dividends.
C. a fixed interest rate.
D. a variable coupon payment.

33. Which of the following is the part of an employee's tax liability that is taken by the employer from wages or salary and paid directly to the government?

A. Wage tax
B. Deferred tax
C. Withholding tax
D. None of the above are correct.

34. A trustee-to-trustee transfer of a retirement plan is also known as a/an:

A. indirect transfer.
B. direct transfer.
C. fiduciary transfer.
D. executive transfer.

35. All but which of the following are methods of calculating the cost basis of a mutual fund investment?

A. FIFO
B. ISO
C. Average cost
D. Specific identification

36. A _______ payment is a large one-time payment made at the end of a loan term in order to retire the debt.

A. fixed
B. serial
C. balloon
D. principal

37. If comparable bonds are yielding 8.8%, what is the current value of a bond with a $1,000 face value, a 6% semiannual coupon, and 5 years until maturity?

A. $888.68
B. $900.97
C. $912.33
D. $922.35

38. When a person dies without leaving a will, he or she dies:

A. aleatory.
B. nuncupative.
C. testate.
D. intestate.

39. Which of the following is the part of Medicare that pays for drug coverage?

A. Part A
B. Part B
C. Part C
D. Part D

40. The retirement plan provision known as a "CODA" is a:

A. certificate of deposit account.
B. cash or deferred arrangement.
C. credit or default arrangement.
D. contribution or deferral account.

41. Which of the following is the total value of assets for which an investment advisor provides certain kinds of investment advice?

A. AMT
B. AUM
C. MAGI
D. NUA

42. The duration of a bond is least affected by its:

A. time to maturity.
B. coupon.
C. quality.
D. interest rate.

43. When is a gift considered to be complete?

A. When the donor relinquishes dominion and control of the property.
B. When the recipient has the right to possess and enjoy the property.
C. When the recipient reports the gift on his or her gift tax return.
D. When the donor intends for the gift to be complete.

44. Enforceable contracts must have which of the following characteristics?

(1) Legally competent parties
(2) Legal purpose
(3) Consideration
(4) Offer and acceptance

A. (3) and (4) only
B. (1), (2), and (4) only
C. (1), (3), and (4) only
D. All of the above are correct.

45. A _______ advisor charges a fee for service and does not receive commissions.

A. hybrid
B. fee-based
C. fee-only
D. broker/dealer

46. Which of the following is not permitted to establish a 403(b) plan for its employees?

A. Private school
B. State government
C. Public school
D. Federal government

47. All but which of the following are correct regarding target date funds?

A. While target date funds aim to reduce risk over time, they are not risk free, even when the target date has been reached.
B. Target date funds provide guaranteed income in retirement and cannot lose money after the target date has been reached.
C. Target date funds are typically structured as a "fund of funds," meaning they invest in other mutual funds rather than individual securities.
D. All of the above are correct.

48. How is the original basis of a newly purchased asset calculated?

A. Cost minus expenses of sale, such as sales tax paid, installation costs, freight charges, and commissions incurred in purchasing the asset.
B. Cost plus expenses of sale, such as sales tax paid, installation costs, freight charges, and commissions incurred in purchasing the asset.
C. Cost only.
D. None of the above are correct.

49. Which of the following is a contract by which one party conveys property to another for a specified time in exchange for a periodic payment?

A. Lease
B. Leaseback
C. Installment
D. Installment purchase

50. Which of the following would be considered a grantor?

A. A person who creates a will.
B. A person who creates an estate.
C. A person who completes a gift.
D. A person who creates a trust.

51. Which of the following is the comprehensive reform law, enacted in 2010, that increased health insurance coverage for the uninsured and implemented reforms to the health insurance market?

A. SECURE Act
B. CARES Act
C. Affordable Care Act
D. Working Families Tax Relief Act

52. Which of the following provides employees with customized retirement plan benefits and may provide benefits in excess of qualified retirement plan limits?

A. Nonqualified deferred compensation plan
B. Qualified deferred compensation plan
C. Defined contribution compensation plan
D. Defined benefit compensation plan

53. Which of the following allows for an unlimited amount of property to be gifted tax-free between U.S. citizen spouses during lifetime or at death?

A. Probate deduction
B. Credit shelter deduction
C. Tenancy deduction
D. Marital deduction

54. Which of the following is a type of cognitive error in behavioral finance that occurs when individuals maintain their existing beliefs or preferences even after receiving contradictory information?

A. Self-attribution bias
B. Conservatism bias
C. Status quo bias
D. Affinity bias

55. Which of the following is a type of debt security that trades on an exchange and provides a return linked to a market index or benchmark?

A. Bond-debenture note
B. Commercial-indexed note
C. Exchange-traded note
D. Annuity-indexed note

56. Which of the following is the Social Security retirement benefit an individual will receive if he or she elects to begin receiving benefits at full retirement age?

A. SSI
B. AIME
C. PIA
D. OASDI

57. Which of the following is more beneficial to a taxpayer in a 28% bracket, a $4,000 deduction or a $1,000 credit?

A. The credit will benefit the taxpayer by an additional $120.
B. The deduction will benefit the taxpayer by an additional $120.
C. The deduction will benefit the taxpayer by an additional $300.
D. The deduction and credit will benefit the taxpayer by the same amount.

58. Car loans, student loans, and mortgages are examples of which of the following?

A. Installment loans
B. Revolving loans
C. Federal loans
D. Secondary loans

For questions 59 – 63, match the investment with the description that follows. Use only one answer per blank. Answers may be used more than once or not at all.

A. Money market fund
B. Corporate bond
C. Common stock
D. Mutual fund
E. Real estate

59. ____ Diversification smooths price volatility, historical above-inflation return, can preserve purchasing power in a portfolio

60. ____ Liquid, easily converted to cash, low default risk, low real return

61. ____ Fixed return, may lose value if not held until maturity, fixed interest payments

62. ____ Not liquid, generally adequate inflation hedge

63. ____ Used to generate income and growth, marketable, historical above-inflation return, can preserve purchasing power in a portfolio

64. Which of the following trusts can be changed, updated, or revoked at any time by the grantor?

A. Living trust following the death of the grantor.
B. Testamentary trust following the death of the grantor.
C. Irrevocable trust
D. Revocable trust

65. Michael purchased a whole life insurance policy several years ago. He has provided the following information related to the policy:

Guaranteed cash value: $90,000
Premiums billed: $80,000
Existing loan: $25,000
Dividends reducing premium: $5,000

What is the current surrender value of Michael's policy?

A. $60,000
B. $65,000
C. $70,000
D. $90,000

66. Amounts remaining in a/an ______ at the end of the plan year will be forfeited as part of the plan's "use it or lose it" feature.

A. GIC
B. TSP
C. HSA
D. FSA

67. Alpha Lending Company's underwriting requirements specify a maximum housing debt-to-income ratio of 28%. If the applicant discloses annual earnings of $75,000, what is the maximum monthly PITI payment the mortgage company will accept?

A. $1,750
B. $1,825
C. $6,250
D. $21,000

68. Liquidity risk is a type of:

A. non-diversifiable risk.
B. default risk.
C. unsystematic risk.
D. systematic risk.

69. With the joint tenants with rights of survivorship (JTWROS) form of property ownership, which of the following will occur if one joint tenant gifts his or her interest in the property to a new owner?

A. The joint tenancy continues, and the new owner has a tenancy by entirety interest.
B. One joint tenant is not permitted to gift his or her interest in the property to a new owner.
C. The joint tenancy is severed, and the new owner has a tenancy in common interest.
D. None of the above are correct.

70. Which of the following is a type of insurance that provides benefits to chronically ill or disabled individuals over an extended period of time?

A. Medigap insurance
B. Long-term care insurance
C. General liability insurance
D. Umbrella insurance

71. Which of the following is correct regarding the gift tax annual exclusion?

A. The gift tax annual exclusion may be used to offset lifetime generation-skipping transfers.
B. The gift tax annual exclusion may be used for future interest gifts.
C. The gift tax annual exclusion may only be used if the donor itemizes deductions.
D. All of the above are correct.

72. Which of the following are permitted investments in an IRA?

(1) Mutual funds
(2) Money market funds
(3) Common stock
(4) Bond funds

A. (3) and (4) only
B. (1), (2), and (3) only
C. (2), (3), and (4) only
D. All of the above are correct.

73. Which of the following is correct regarding itemized deductions?

A. A taxpayer should itemize deductions if the total allowable deductions are lower than the standard deduction amount.
B. A taxpayer should itemize deductions if the total allowable deductions are higher than the standard deduction amount.
C. A taxpayer should itemize deductions and also take the standard deduction in the same year if they have a large amount of deductions.
D. Itemized deductions are added to a taxpayer's AGI to increase the amount of income that is taxed.

74. Which of the following is an irrevocable refusal to accept a gift, bequest, devise, or legacy left by a decedent?

A. Qualified disclaimer
B. Qualified bequest
C. Reverse gift
D. None of the above are correct.

75. **Which of the following calculates the impact on a bond's yield if it's called prior to maturity and should be performed using the first date on which the issuer could call the bond?**

A. Duration
B. Yield to maturity
C. Yield to call
D. Bond rating

ANSWER KEY

1. D
A sole proprietorship is the simplest form of business entity and has no formal legal requirements. It provides unlimited liability for the owner.

2. B
A car loan payment would appear on the cash flow statement.

3. A
With an irrevocable beneficiary designation, the policyholder does not retain the right to change the beneficiary without restriction.

4. D
A will codicil is suitable for a minor will revision such as changing a specific bequest or updating a beneficiary's legal name due to marriage or divorce. If a testator is legally competent, he or she may execute a will codicil.

5. B
A high estimated inflation rate will require allocating more dollars toward achieving the goal.

6. D
Contributions to a SEP IRA vest immediately.

7. C
A prospectus is a written document that provides all material information about an offering of securities and is the primary sales tool of the company that issues the securities.

8. A
Types of partnerships include general partnerships, limited partnerships, and limited liability partnerships.

9. B
A qualified plan is any retirement plan that meets the applicable requirements of the Internal Revenue Code for tax-favored treatment.

10. A
A testamentary trust may be used to reduce estate taxes, provide professional investment management, and ensure property in a decedent's estate is passed according to the decedent's wishes. A testamentary trust does not avoid probate.

11. C
After understanding the client's personal and financial circumstances, the next step of the financial planning process is identifying and selecting goals.

12. B
TIPS are Treasury inflation-protected securities whose principal increases with inflation and decreases with deflation. They are issued by the United States Treasury.

13. A
The six parts of the personal automobile policy (PAP) are:
Part A: Liability coverage
Part B: Medical payments coverage
Part C: Uninsured motorist coverage
Part D: Coverage for damage to your automobile
Part E: Duties after an accident or loss
Part F: General provisions

14. A
Employer contributions to a defined contribution plan must use either the 3-year cliff vesting or 6-year graded vesting schedules.

15. D
Blue chip stocks represent highly regarded, well-established companies that have demonstrated the ability to operate profitably in both positive and negative economic climates.

16. C
The percentage of taxable income that an individual pays in taxes is the effective tax rate.

17. A
Alimony payments, government loans, and child support payments are not dischargeable through bankruptcy.

18. B
A life estate is a type of joint ownership of real property in which ownership is split between a present interest and a remainder interest.

19. B
Total risk = systematic risk + unsystematic risk.
This formula can be rewritten as: Total risk – systematic risk = unsystematic risk.

20. C
Variable life insurance is a type of permanent insurance in which the cash value and death benefit vary according to the value of underlying investments selected by the insured.

21. B
COBRA continuation coverage is provided to employees who are voluntarily or involuntarily terminated for reasons except gross misconduct.

22. D
An individual who creates a last will and testament is known as a testator.

23. C
Relating to the time value of money, a serial payment increases each period to keep up with inflation.

24. D
The conversion provision in a life insurance policy allows an insured to convert from term insurance to permanent insurance without having to show evidence of insurability.

25. C
$4\% \times -1.2 = -4.8\%$
A stock with a beta of –1.2 will move 120% in the opposite direction of the market. If the stock market increases by 4%, the stock will decrease by 4.8%.

26. A
Medicaid is a needs-based social welfare program that provides benefits to low-income adults, their families, and individuals with certain disabilities.

27. B
A first-time home purchase up to $10,000 and qualified education expenses for the account owner's child are among the exemptions from the 10% early withdrawal penalty from an IRA. Hardship withdrawals are permitted in 401(k) plans but not IRAs. Loans from IRAs are not allowed.

28. B
The Truth in Lending Act (TILA) protects consumers against inaccurate and unfair credit card practices and requires lenders to provide loan cost information so that consumers can comparison shop for certain types of loans.

29. A
If an investor uses dollar cost averaging, more shares of an investment will be purchased when the share price is low and fewer shares when the share price is high.

30. D
Property acquired by either spouse prior to marriage, as well as property acquired by either spouse during marriage by gift or inheritance are not considered community property. They are separate property.

31. A
Cross-purchase and entity-purchase are types of buy-sell agreements.

32. B
Equity income mutual funds generally invest in stocks that pay above average dividends.

33. C
Withholding tax is the part of an employee's tax liability that is taken by the employer from wages or salary and paid directly to the government.

34. B
A trustee-to-trustee transfer of a retirement plan is also known as a direct transfer.

35. B
FIFO (first in, first out), average cost, and specific identification are methods of calculating the cost basis of a mutual fund investment.

36. C
A balloon payment is a large one-time payment made at the end of a loan term in order to retire the debt.

37. A
FV = $1,000
i = 8.8 / 2 = 4.4
n = 5 × 2 = 10
PMT = $1,000 × 0.06 = $60, then $60 / 2 = $30
PV = ? = $888.68

38. D
When a person dies without leaving a will, he or she dies intestate.

39. D
The part of Medicare that pays for drug coverage is Part D.

40. B
The retirement plan provision known as a "CODA" is a cash or deferred arrangement.

41. B
AUM (assets under management) is the total value of assets for which an investment advisor provides certain kinds of investment advice.

42. C
There is an inverse relationship between interest rates, coupon payments, and duration. As interest rates and coupon payments decrease, duration increases. There is a direct relationship between time to maturity and duration. The longer the time to maturity, the longer the duration. A bond's quality does not directly impact its duration.

43. A
A gift is complete when the donor relinquishes dominion and control of the property.

44. D
Enforceable contracts must have legally competent parties, a legal purpose, consideration, and offer and acceptance.

45. C
A fee-only advisor charges a fee for service and does not receive commissions.

46. D
A 403(b) plan may be adopted by an employer that is a state, agency of a state, nonprofit organization, public university, or private university.

47. B
Target date funds do not provide guaranteed income in retirement and can lose money if the underlying investments owned by the fund decrease in value. While target date funds aim to reduce risk over time, they are not risk free, even when the target date has been reached. Target date funds are typically structured as a "fund of funds," meaning they invest in other mutual funds rather than individual securities.

48. B
The original basis of a newly purchased asset is equal to the cost plus expenses of sale, such as sales tax paid, installation costs, freight charges, and commissions incurred in purchasing the asset.

49. A
A lease is a contract by which one party conveys property to another for a specified time in exchange for a periodic payment.

50. D
A grantor is a person who creates a trust.

51. C
The Affordable Care Act (ACA) is the comprehensive reform law, enacted in 2010, that increased health insurance coverage for the uninsured and implemented reforms to the health insurance market.

52. A
A nonqualified deferred compensation plan provides employees with customized retirement plan benefits and may provide benefits in excess of qualified retirement plan limits.

53. D
The marital deduction allows for an unlimited amount of property to be gifted tax-free between U.S. citizen spouses during lifetime or at death.

54. B
Conservatism bias is a type of cognitive error in behavioral finance that occurs when individuals maintain their existing beliefs or preferences even after receiving contradictory information.

55. C
An exchange-traded note (ETN) is a type of debt security that trades on an exchange and provides a return linked to a market index or benchmark.

56. C
The PIA (primary insurance amount) is the Social Security retirement benefit an individual will receive if he or she elects to begin receiving benefits at full retirement age.

57. B
Step 1: $4,000 × 0.28 = $1,120
Step 2: $1,120 – $1,000 = $120
The deduction is more beneficial because it creates the equivalent of a $1,120 credit, which is $120 more than the $1,000 credit.

58. A
Car loans, student loans, and mortgages are examples of installment loans.

59. D
Mutual fund: Diversification smooths price volatility, historical above-inflation return, can preserve purchasing power in a portfolio

60. A
Money market fund: Liquid, easily converted to cash, low default risk, low real return

61. B
Corporate bond: Fixed return, may lose value if not held until maturity, fixed interest payments

62. E
Real estate: Not liquid, generally adequate inflation hedge

63. C
Common stock: Used to generate income and growth, marketable, historical above-inflation return, can preserve purchasing power in a portfolio

64. D
A revocable trust can be changed, updated, or revoked at any time by the grantor.

65. B
Surrender value = \$90,000 – \$25,000 = \$65,000

66. D
Amounts remaining in an FSA (flexible spending account) at the end of the plan year will be forfeited as part of the plan's "use it or lose it" feature.

67. A
Step 1: Maximum annual PITI = \$75,000 × 0.28 = \$21,000
Step 2: Maximum monthly PITI = \$21,000 / 12 months = \$1,750

68. C
Liquidity risk is a type of unsystematic risk.

69. C
With the joint tenants with rights of survivorship (JTWROS) form of property ownership, if one joint tenant gifts his or her interest in the property to a new owner then the joint tenancy is severed, and the new owner has a tenancy in common interest.

70. B
Long-term care insurance provides benefits to chronically ill or disabled individuals over an extended period of time.

71. A
The gift tax annual exclusion may be used to offset lifetime generation-skipping transfers.

72. D
Mutual funds, money market funds, common stock, and bond funds are all permitted investments in an IRA.

73. B
A taxpayer should itemize deductions if the total allowable deductions are higher than the standard deduction amount.

74. A

A qualified disclaimer is an irrevocable refusal to accept a gift, bequest, devise, or legacy left by a decedent.

75. C

Yield to call calculates the impact on a bond's yield if it's called prior to maturity and should be performed using the first date on which the issuer could call the bond.

PRACTICE EXAM 2

QUESTIONS

1. A provision in a life insurance policy that prevents an insurer from revoking coverage because of alleged misstatements by an insured after a specified period, usually two years, is referred to as a/an:

A. incontestable clause.
B. indemnity clause.
C. misstatement of age clause.
D. statute of frauds clause.

2. Which of the following is/are correct regarding open-end mutual funds?

(1) Open-end mutual funds sell at their net asset value (NAV).
(2) Open-end mutual funds have a fixed capital structure.

A. (1) only
B. (2) only
C. None of the above are correct.
D. All of the above are correct.

3. Which of the following is considered a non-taxable gift and does not require payment of gift tax?

A. A gift that does not exceed the gift tax annual exclusion.
B. A gift to charity.
C. A gift to a political organization.
D. All of the above are correct.

4. Which of the following are the two forms of vesting that employer contributions may be subject to in a retirement plan?

A. Taxable vesting and tax-exempt vesting
B. Graded vesting and cliff vesting
C. Simple vesting and compound vesting
D. Qualified vesting and nonqualified vesting

5. Which of the following is the formula to calculate an individual's net worth?

A. Net worth = assets + liabilities
B. Net worth = assets – liabilities
C. Net worth = liabilities – assets
D. None of the above are correct.

6. All but which of the following are correct regarding a bond's call provision?

A. It protects the issuer from declines in interest rates.
B. It may be included in a bond agreement.
C. It will cause the investor's required rate of return to be lower.
D. It allows the issuer to redeem the bond early.

7. Mary, age 67, recently received a $650,000 inheritance from her uncle's estate. To provide sufficient income during retirement, she needs an annuity that will produce the highest payout for the rest of her life. Which settlement option should Mary select?

A. Dollar certain
B. Joint life
C. Single life
D. Life with a 10-year period certain

8. Which of the following are reported on Schedule D of IRS Form 1040?

A. Capital gains and losses
B. Itemized deductions
C. Interest and ordinary dividends
D. Profit or loss from business

9. Umbrella insurance policies generally have a ______ minimum and can be purchased in ______ dollar increments.

A. $1,000; thousand
B. $10,000; million
C. $1,000,000; thousand
D. $1,000,000; million

10. Which of the following is correct concerning the risk of smoking a cigar indoors?

(1) Smoking a cigar indoors is a hazard.
(2) Smoking a cigar indoors is a peril.
(3) A fire that results from smoking indoors is a hazard.
(4) A fire that results from smoking indoors is a peril.

A. (1) and (3) only
B. (1) and (4) only
C. (2) and (3) only
D. (3) and (4) only

11. In order to maintain a SIMPLE plan, an employer may not have more than ______ employees.

A. 25
B. 50
C. 75
D. 100

12. Exchange rate risk is also known as which of the following?

A. Currency risk
B. Liquidity risk
C. Reinvestment risk
D. Interest rate risk

13. Carol is concerned about maintaining her privacy and wants to avoid probate at death. Which of her assets would be subject to probate?

(1) A condo she owns in common with her husband.
(2) An annuity that names her sister as beneficiary.
(3) Land owned jointly (JTWROS) with her daughter that Carol contributed all the money to purchase.
(4) Her sole proprietorship business.

A. (1) and (3) only
B. (1) and (4) only
C. (2) and (3) only
D. (2) and (4) only

14. Phil owns an investment yielding a 10% pre-tax return. If he is in the 25% tax bracket, what is the equivalent after-tax return?

A. 7.2%
B. 7.5%
C. 13.3%
D. 13.8%

15. If an insured borrows a portion of the cash value from a whole life policy, which of the following is correct?

A. Any outstanding policy loans must be deducted from the face amount of the policy before the death benefit is paid.
B. Any outstanding policy loans will be added to the face amount of the policy before the death benefit is paid.
C. Outstanding policy loans have no effect on the face amount of the policy or the death benefit that will be paid.
D. Outstanding policy loans must be repaid by the beneficiary after the death benefit has been paid out.

16. The U.S. government agency known as the "PBGC" is the:

A. Public Budget Governance Commission.
B. Pension Bankruptcy Governance Commission.
C. Pension Benefit Guaranty Corporation.
D. Private Bankruptcy Government Charter.

17. Consumer debt payments, such as credit cards and vehicle loans, should not exceed _______ of net income.

A. 15%
B. 20%
C. 25%
D. 36%

18. Which of the following is a payroll tax imposed by the federal government to fund Social Security and Medicare benefits?

A. AMT tax
B. Corporate tax
C. FUTA tax
D. FICA tax

19. A living will may also be referred to as which of the following?

A. Inter-vivos trust
B. Will codicil
C. Advance medical directive
D. Durable power of attorney

20. Which of the following is not one of the three basic types of investment companies?

A. Open-end funds
B. Closed-end funds
C. Guaranteed investment contracts
D. Unit investment trusts

21. All but which of the following are potential risks of borrowing money through a home equity line of credit?

A. The interest rate is typically variable, which may lead to higher payments over time.
B. Because the line of credit is linked to the performance of underlying investments, it may decrease over time.
C. Defaulting on the line of credit may allow the lender to foreclose on the property.
D. The monthly payment may fluctuate which can make budgeting difficult.

22. Generally, only employers contribute to which of the following retirement plans?

A. Defined benefit plan
B. Defined contribution plan
C. Traditional IRA
D. Roth IRA

23. Which of the following is a tax-advantaged savings plan that is intended to be used to pay for a beneficiary's qualified education expenses?

A. 457 plan
B. 529 plan
C. 1031 plan
D. 1035 plan

24. Which of the following is the ability to buy or sell an investment quickly and at a known price without incurring a significant loss of value?

A. Marketability
B. Transferability
C. Convertibility
D. Liquidity

25. Which of the following refers to a surviving spouse's right to opt for the statutorily defined portion of a deceased spouse's estate, rather than through the provisions made in the will?

A. Spousal election
B. Spousal credit
C. Marital deduction
D. Survival exemption

26. Erin has taxable income of $200,000 and a tax liability of $55,000. Tom has taxable income of $150,000 and a tax liability of $35,000. The tax rate structure being used to tax Erin and Tom is:

A. proportional.
B. value added.
C. progressive.
D. flat.

27. A _______ is any person engaged in the business of buying or selling securities for the account of others. A _______ is any person engaged in the business of buying or selling securities, but for their own account.

A. dealer; broker
B. broker; dealer
C. trustee; fiduciary
D. fiduciary; trustee

28. A photographer can no longer afford to replace his expensive camera that is constantly being damaged on photo shoots. He decides to only edit photos rather than take pictures. Which method of risk management is the photographer using?

A. Transfer
B. Reduction
C. Avoidance
D. Retention

29. Which of the following is money that an employer contributes to an employee's retirement account, typically based on the employee's contribution and capped at a certain percentage of income?

A. Matching contribution
B. Deferred contribution
C. Graded vesting contribution
D. Elective deferral contribution

30. Which of the following financial principles states that a sum of money today is worth more than the same sum of money will be worth in the future?

A. Modern portfolio theory
B. Capital asset pricing model
C. Time value of money
D. Efficient market hypothesis

31. Which of the following is the price that an investor pays to purchase an open-end mutual fund?

A. APY
B. EPS
C. IRR
D. NAV

32. Which of the following is a tax on the transfer of property at death?

A. Federal transfer tax
B. Federal estate tax
C. Adjusted estate tax
D. Tentative transfer tax

33. All but which of the following are types of annuity settlement options?

A. Single life
B. Installment refund
C. Life with period certain
D. Extended term

For questions 34 – 37, choose the correct tax treatment for the items listed. Use only one answer per blank. Answers may be used more than once or not at all.

A. Included in income
B. Excluded from income

34. ____ Rental income

35. ____ Life insurance death benefit

36. ____ Royalties

37. ____ Income earned on inherited property

38. All but which of the following requirements must be met to qualify for a health savings account (HSA)?

A. The participant must not be enrolled in Medicare.
B. The participant cannot be claimed as a dependent by another taxpayer.
C. The participant must not be covered under a high deductible health plan.
D. All of the above are correct.

39. Which of the following conveys an individual's current financial status and is numerical in nature?

A. Qualitative data
B. Quantitative data
C. Subjective data
D. Categorical data

40. Which of the following is a method used to determine the approximate length of time it takes for an investment to double in value?

A. Dividend growth model
B. Rule of 72
C. Exponential growth rule
D. Capital asset pricing model

41. All but which of the following are correct regarding probate?

A. It provides for clean title to a decedent's property.
B. It is the process by which a state or local court validates the will of a decedent.
C. It protects the decedent from an untimely filing of claims by his or her lifetime creditors.
D. It may be either a public or private process depending on the decedent's wishes.

42. Which of the following is a method for valuing an insured's home that uses the cost to rebuild or replace the structure with new property of like kind and quality, minus depreciation?

A. Actual cash value
B. Substitute cost value
C. Replacement cost value
D. Depreciation cash value

43. Which of the following can be used to measure investment risk?

A. Sharpe ratio
B. Standard deviation
C. Beta
D. All of the above are correct.

44. Business partnerships use ______ to report to the IRS a partner's share of income, deductions, and credits.

A. Form 1099
B. Form K-1
C. Form W-2
D. Form W-9

45. Which of the following are correct regarding Roth IRAs?

(1) Contributions to a Roth IRA can be made at any age.
(2) Contributions to a Roth IRA must be made before age 72.
(3) A Roth IRA owner is not required to take a required minimum distribution during his or her lifetime.
(4) Roth IRA contributions may be deducted in limited circumstances.

A. (1) and (3) only
B. (2) and (3) only
C. (1), (3), and (4) only
D. (2), (3), and (4) only

46. Which of the following is the price of property that would be agreed upon between a willing buyer and a willing seller, with neither party being required to act, and both having reasonable knowledge of the relevant facts?

A. Intrinsic value
B. Liquidation value
C. Fair market value
D. Investment value

47. Financial risk is a type of:

A. market risk.
B. systematic risk.
C. unsystematic risk.
D. purchasing power risk.

48. For a revocable living trust, which of the following occurs at the grantor's death?

A. The trust becomes revocable, avoids probate, and assets pass to designated beneficiaries.
B. The trust becomes irrevocable, goes to probate, and assets pass to designated beneficiaries.
C. The trust becomes revocable, goes to probate, and assets pass to designated beneficiaries.
D. The trust becomes irrevocable, avoids probate, and assets pass to designated beneficiaries.

49. Which of the following clauses allows an insurer to defer the payment of policy benefits to a beneficiary for a specified period of time after the death of the insured under certain conditions?

A. Delay clause
B. Incontestability clause
C. Spendthrift clause
D. Grace period clause

50. Common stock generates income and growth for investors through:

A. interest and depreciation.
B. coupon payments and stock splits.
C. capital gain distributions and inflation.
D. dividends and capital appreciation.

51. In a SWOT analysis, the "W" stands for:

A. workflows.
B. weaknesses.
C. worries.
D. withdrawals.

52. The inverse relationship between bond prices and an investor's required rate of return is known as:

A. credit risk.
B. liquidity risk.
C. reinvestment risk.
D. interest rate risk.

53. Robert purchased a rare coin for $600. He kept the coin for 5 years before selling it. If the internal rate of return for the 5-year period was 9%, what was the final selling price?

A. $923.17
B. $926.39
C. $930.28
D. $933.40

54. Mirroring and active listening are forms of ______ between an advisor and client.

A. cognitive errors
B. emotional biases
C. interpersonal communication
D. qualitative data

55. Which of the following is/are correct regarding gift splitting?

(1) Gift splitting may be used on a gift-by-gift basis during a calendar year.
(2) Both spouses must consent to the use of gift splitting. However, if no gift tax is due then a gift tax return is not necessary.

A. (1) only
B. (2) only
C. None of the above are correct.
D. All of the above are correct.

56. Which of the following is the amount of interest paid to a bond investor and is calculated by multiplying the interest of a bond by its face value?

A. Coupon payment
B. Call payment
C. Principal payment
D. Inflation payment

57. Decreasing term life insurance is characterized by a ______ premium and ______ face amount of coverage.

A. decreasing; increasing
B. decreasing; decreasing
C. level; decreasing
D. decreasing; level

58. For determining eligibility to receive Social Security retirement benefits, a maximum of ______ credits (quarters of coverage) may be earned in a single calendar year.

A. 2
B. 4
C. 6
D. 8

59. A/An ______ student loan is distributed on the basis of financial need and interest is not charged to the student while he or she is enrolled in school at least half time.

A. consolidated
B. income-based
C. unsubsidized
D. subsidized

60. All but which of the following are types of REITs?

A. Hybrid REIT
B. Commercial REIT
C. Mortgage REIT
D. Equity REIT

61. In estate planning, GSTT is an abbreviation for which of the following?

A. Generation-skipping transfer tax
B. Grantor's-standard transfer tax
C. Gift-skipping testamentary trust
D. Generation-skipping testamentary trust

62. Which of the following measures the number of deaths in a specific population over a period of time and is used by life insurance issuers to calculate the premiums they charge?

A. Morbidity rate
B. Comorbidity rate
C. Mortality rate
D. None of the above are correct.

63. A bond that was issued with a face value of $1,000 that is currently trading for ______ is considered a premium bond.

A. $0
B. $975
C. $1,000
D. $1,025

64. FINRA regulates which of the following?

A. Registered Investment Advisors and accredited investors
B. Credit lenders and transfer agents
C. Broker-dealer firms and registered brokers
D. Stock exchanges and clearing agencies

65. Zack reports the following transactions for the current year:

Earned a salary of $80,000 through his full-time job.
Schedule C loss of $6,000.
Received a $30,000 inheritance due to his uncle's death.

What is Zack's gross income for the current year?

A. $44,000
B. $74,000
C. $80,000
D. $104,000

66. All but which of the following are correct regarding 401(k) plans?

A. An employer may contribute to an employee's 401(k) account and offer a matching contribution.
B. In-service withdrawals from a 401(k) plan are subject to a 20% premature distribution penalty for employees under age 72.
C. There is a dollar limit on the amount an employee may elect to defer to a 401(k) account each year.
D. All of the above are correct.

67. How are the death benefits of a modified endowment contract (MEC) taxed?

A. They are taxed as ordinary income to the beneficiary.
B. They are taxed at capital gains rates to the beneficiary.
C. They are taxed partly as ordinary income and partly as capital gains.
D. The death benefits are tax-free (same as a non-MEC).

68. Which of the following is correct regarding completed gifts?

A. Gifts of a future interest are eligible for the gift tax annual exclusion.
B. Any consideration received by a donor will increase the value of the gift.
C. Gifts may be split between spouses, thereby doubling the amount of property that may be gifted without gift tax liability to any number of donees.
D. A gift made directly to an educational institution or medical care provider on behalf of another individual will be treated as a taxable gift.

69. Which of the following is a commonly used retirement plan for small businesses because of its simplicity and low administrative costs?

A. 457 plan
B. SEP
C. Thrift savings plan
D. None of the above are correct.

70. All but which of the following are types of mortgages?

A. Fixed-rate mortgage
B. Reverse mortgage
C. Interest-only mortgage
D. Credit mortgage

71. The fixed income investment known as a "CD" is a:

A. certificate of deposit.
B. credit default swap.
C. cash dividend.
D. collateralized debt obligation.

72. Which of the following is/are correct regarding a preferred provider organization (PPO)?

(1) It is a type of health plan where the insured pays less if a provider in the plan's network is used.
(2) An insured can use doctors, hospitals, and providers outside the network without a referral for an additional cost.

A. (1) only
B. (2) only
C. None of the above are correct.
D. All of the above are correct.

73. All but which of the following can be used to reduce risk in an investment portfolio?

A. Diversifying investments across sectors.
B. Increasing the concentration of investments.
C. Using a broad asset allocation strategy.
D. Rebalancing the portfolio on a periodic basis.

74. Which of the following is an investment's rate of return after adjusting for inflation?

A. Nominal return
B. Real return
C. Internal rate of return
D. Holding period return

75. All but which of the following are correct regarding the tenancy by entirety form of property ownership?

A. It is an interest in property that can be held only by spouses.
B. The property automatically passes to the surviving spouse when one spouse dies.
C. It is an interest in property that can be held by non-spouses in an incorporated business.
D. In most states, it is not severable by an individual spouse.

ANSWER KEY

1. A
A provision in a life insurance policy that prevents an insurer from revoking coverage because of alleged misstatements by an insured after a specified period, usually two years, is referred to as an incontestable clause.

2. A
Open-end mutual funds sell at their net asset value (NAV). Only closed-end mutual funds have a fixed capital structure.

3. D
Gifts to charity, gifts to a political organization, and gifts that do not exceed the gift tax annual exclusion are considered non-taxable gifts and do not require payment of gift tax.

4. B
The two forms of vesting that employer contributions may be subject to in a retirement plan are graded vesting and cliff vesting.

5. B
The formula to calculate an individual's net worth is: Net worth = assets – liabilities

6. C
A bond's call provision protects the issuer from declines in interest rates by allowing the issuer to redeem the bond early. A call provision may be included in a bond agreement. If a bond is callable, it will cause an investor's required rate of return to be higher due to the increased risk.

7. C
A single life annuity will provide the maximum payout to Mary. A single life annuity is also referred to as a pure life annuity.

8. A
Capital gains and losses are reported on Schedule D of IRS Form 1040.

9. D
Umbrella insurance policies generally have a $1,000,000 minimum and can be purchased in million dollar increments.

10. B
Smoking a cigar indoors (hazard) increases the chance that a loss from a fire (peril) will occur.

11. D
In order to maintain a SIMPLE plan, an employer may not have more than 100 employees.

12. A
Exchange rate risk is also known as currency risk.

13. B
The condo that Carol owns in common with her husband, as well as Carol's sole proprietorship business would be subject to probate.

14. B
After-tax return = $0.1 \times (1 - 0.25) = 7.5\%$

15. A
If an insured borrows a portion of the cash value from a whole life policy, then any outstanding policy loans must be deducted from the face amount of the policy before the death benefit is paid.

16. C
The U.S. government agency known as the "PBGC" is the Pension Benefit Guaranty Corporation.

17. B
Consumer debt payments, such as credit cards and vehicle loans, should not exceed 20% of net income.

18. D
FICA tax is a payroll tax imposed by the federal government to fund Social Security and Medicare benefits.

19. C
A living will may also be referred to as an advance medical directive.

20. C
The three basic types of investment companies are open-end funds, closed-end funds, and unit investment trusts.

21. B
The interest rate of a home equity line of credit is typically variable, which may lead to higher payments over time. Because the monthly payment may fluctuate, it can make budgeting difficult. Defaulting on the line of credit may allow the lender to foreclose on the property. A home equity line of credit is not linked to the performance of underlying investments.

22. A
Generally, only employers contribute to defined benefit plans.

23. B
A 529 plan is a tax-advantaged savings plan that is intended to be used to pay for a beneficiary's qualified education expenses.

24. D
Liquidity is the ability to buy or sell an investment quickly and at a known price without incurring a significant loss of value.

25. A
Spousal election refers to a surviving spouse's right to opt for the statutorily defined portion of a deceased spouse's estate, rather than through the provisions made in the will.

26. C
The tax rate structure being used to tax Erin and Tom is progressive. A progressive tax structure takes a larger percentage of income from high-income earners than from low-income earners.

27. B
A broker is any person engaged in the business of buying or selling securities for the account of others. A dealer is any person engaged in the business of buying or selling securities, but for their own account.

28. C
The photographer is avoiding the risk that damage will occur to his camera by no longer taking pictures.

29. A
A matching contribution is money that an employer contributes to an employee's retirement account, typically based on the employee's contribution and capped at a certain percentage of income.

30. C
Time value of money is the financial principle that states that a sum of money today is worth more than the same sum of money will be worth in the future.

31. D
The price that an investor pays to purchase an open-end mutual fund is the NAV (net asset value).

32. B
Federal estate tax is a tax on the transfer of property at death.

33. D
The annuity settlement options are cash, single life, life with period certain, joint-and-survivor, and installment refund.

34. A
Rental income is included in income.

35. B
Life insurance death benefit is excluded from income.

36. A
Royalties are included in income.

37. A
Income earned on inherited property is included in income.

38. C
To qualify for a health savings account (HSA), the participant must be covered under a compatible high deductible health plan, must not be enrolled in Medicare, and cannot be claimed as a dependent by another taxpayer.

39. B
Quantitative data conveys an individual's current financial status and is numerical in nature.

40. B
The rule of 72 is a method used to determine the approximate length of time it takes for an investment to double in value.

41. D
Probate is the process by which a state or local court validates the will of a decedent. It provides for clean title to a decedent's property and protects a decedent from an untimely filing of claims by his or her lifetime creditors. Probate is a public process.

42. A
Actual cash value is a method for valuing an insured's home that uses the cost to rebuild or replace the structure with new property of like kind and quality, minus depreciation.

43. D
Sharpe ratio, standard deviation, and beta can be used to measure investment risk.

44. B
Business partnerships use Form K-1 to report to the IRS a partner's share of income, deductions, and credits.

45. A
Contributions to a Roth IRA can be made at any age and are never deductible. A Roth IRA owner is not required to take a required minimum distribution during his or her lifetime.

46. C
Fair market value is the price of property that would be agreed upon between a willing buyer and a willing seller, with neither party being required to act, and both having reasonable knowledge of the relevant facts.

47. C
Financial risk is a type of unsystematic risk.

48. D
At the grantor's death, a revocable living trust becomes irrevocable, avoids probate, and assets pass to designated beneficiaries.

49. A
A delay clause allows an insurer to defer the payment of policy benefits to a beneficiary for a specified period of time after the death of the insured under certain conditions.

50. D
Common stock generates income and growth for investors through dividends and capital appreciation.

51. B
In a SWOT analysis, the "W" stands for weaknesses.

52. D
Interest rate risk is the risk that, as interest rates rise, bond prices will fall. Interest rate risk is measured by a bond's duration.

53. A
PV = -$600
n = 5
i = 9
PMT = 0
FV = ? = $923.17

54. C
Mirroring and active listening are forms of interpersonal communication between an advisor and client.

55. C
If spouses split one gift in a calendar year, all gifts must be split. Even if no gift tax is due, a gift tax return must still be filed.

56. A
A coupon payment is the amount of interest paid to a bond investor and is calculated by multiplying the interest of a bond by its face value.

57. C
Decreasing term life insurance is characterized by a level premium and decreasing face amount of coverage.

58. B
For determining eligibility to receive Social Security retirement benefits, a maximum of 4 credits (quarters of coverage) may be earned in a single calendar year.

59. D
A subsidized student loan is distributed on the basis of financial need and interest is not charged to the student while he or she is enrolled in school at least half time.

60. B
The three types of REITs are equity REITs, mortgage REITs, and hybrid REITs.

61. A
In estate planning, GSTT is an abbreviation for generation-skipping transfer tax.

62. C
Mortality rate measures the number of deaths in a specific population over a period of time and is used by life insurance issuers to calculate the premiums they charge.

63. D
A bond that was issued with a face value of $1,000 that is currently trading for $1,025 is considered a premium bond.

64. C
FINRA regulates broker-dealer firms and registered brokers.

65. B
$80,000 – $6,000 = $74,000
Zack's salary of $80,000 is reduced by the $6,000 Schedule C loss. The inheritance is not included in Zack's gross income.

66. B
In-service withdrawals from a 401(k) plan are subject to a 10% premature distribution penalty for employees under age 59 ½. An employer may contribute to an employee's 401(k) account and offer a matching contribution, and there is a dollar limit on the amount an employee may elect to defer to a 401(k) account each year.

67. D
The death benefits of a modified endowment contract (MEC) are tax-free (same as a non-MEC).

68. C
Gifts of a present interest, not a future interest, are eligible for the gift tax annual exclusion. Any consideration received by a donor will decrease the value of the gift. A gift made directly to an educational institution or medical care provider on behalf of another individual will be treated as a non-taxable gift. Gifts may be split between spouses, thereby doubling the amount of property that may be gifted without gift tax liability to any number of donees.

69. B
A SEP is a commonly used retirement plan for small businesses because of its simplicity and low administrative costs.

70. D
Types of mortgages include fixed-rate mortgages, reverse mortgages, and interest-only mortgages.

71. A
The fixed income investment known as a "CD" is a certificate of deposit.

72. D
A preferred provider organization (PPO) is a type of health plan where the insured pays less if a provider in the plan's network is used. An insured can use doctors, hospitals, and providers outside the network without a referral for an additional cost.

73. B
Diversifying investments across sectors, using a broad asset allocation strategy, and rebalancing the portfolio on a periodic basis can all be used to reduce risk in a portfolio. Increasing the concentration of investments would increase risk, not reduce it.

74. B
An investment's rate of return after adjusting for inflation is its real return.

75. C
Tenancy by entirety is an interest in property that can be held only by spouses. The property automatically passes to the surviving spouse when one spouse dies. In most states, it is not severable by an individual spouse.

PRACTICE EXAM 3

QUESTIONS

1. Megan, age 60, is listed as beneficiary of her brother's $350,000 life insurance policy. Megan is single and in the 20% tax bracket. If her brother were to die, how much tax would Megan owe?

   A. $0
   B. $35,000
   C. $70,000
   D. $105,000

2. All but which of the following are considered cash equivalents?

   A. Treasury bills
   B. Commercial paper
   C. Money market funds
   D. Commodities

3. Which of the following vesting schedules may apply to employee contributions to a defined contribution retirement plan?

   A. Cliff vesting
   B. Graded vesting
   C. Immediate vesting
   D. All of the above are correct.

4. The balance sheet is also referred to as which of the following?

   A. Cash flow statement
   B. Income statement
   C. Profit and loss statement
   D. Statement of financial position

5. Which of the following involves using debt to increase an investment's expected return?

   A. Leveraging
   B. Hedging
   C. Indexing
   D. Diversifying

6. Which of the following is a tax on the transfer of property by one individual to another while receiving nothing, or less than full value, in return?

   A. Estate tax
   B. Probate tax
   C. Testamentary tax
   D. Gift tax

7. All but which of the following are correct regarding reverse mortgages?

A. It allows a homeowner to borrow money using the home as security for the loan.
B. With a reverse mortgage, the borrower does not make monthly mortgage payments.
C. When a homeowner takes out a reverse mortgage, the title to the home is transferred out of the borrower's name.
D. All of the above are correct.

8. In most states, if an insured commits suicide within the first two years after a life insurance policy is issued, which of the following will result?

A. No death benefit will be paid.
B. The full death benefit will be paid.
C. The insurance company will pay only the cumulative premiums plus interest earned.
D. None of the above are correct.

9. The type of investment known as a "REIT" is a:

A. registered earned income trust.
B. real estate investment trust.
C. Roth executive income trust.
D. registered exchange indexed trust.

10. Which of the following is/are correct regarding COBRA continuation coverage?

(1) It is not available to children of a covered employee who lose coverage due to age limitations or marriage.
(2) It must be identical to coverage provided to employees, apart from cost.

A. (1) only
B. (2) only
C. None of the above are correct.
D. All of the above are correct.

11. Which of the following is a type of cognitive error in behavioral finance that occurs when individuals view their wealth and income in nominal terms instead of inflation-adjusted terms?

A. Mental accounting
B. Self-attribution bias
C. Money illusion
D. Illusion of control

12. TIPS are intended to protect investors against which of the following?

A. Market risk
B. Inflation risk
C. Political risk
D. Currency risk

13. Which of the following is the legal process that determines the order of priority in which heirs would receive property if a decedent died without a valid will?

A. Testamentary order
B. Intestate succession
C. Statutory progression
D. Testate provisions

14. Which of the following is correct regarding UGMA and UTMA accounts?

A. Donors can make revocable contributions up to $2,000 per year into an UGMA or UTMA account.
B. Assets in an UGMA or UTMA account become available to the minor when he or she reaches the age of the majority.
C. UGMA and UTMA accounts are tax-exempt and are not subject to kiddie tax rules.
D. None of the above are correct.

15. Which of the following is the percentage of costs of a covered health care service that an insured must pay (20%, for example) after having paid the deductible?

A. Stop-loss
B. Premium
C. Indemnity
D. Coinsurance

16. Which of the following occurs to an employee's non-vested account balance if employment is terminated?

A. It will be forfeited.
B. It will be paid out as cash.
C. It will be rolled over to an IRA.
D. It will be rolled into a nonqualified plan.

17. Which of the following theories is based on the assumption that investors are risk averse, and for a given level of risk investors prefer higher returns to lower returns?

A. Capital asset pricing theory
B. Dividend discount model theory
C. Modern portfolio theory
D. Efficient market theory

18. Which of the following is the distribution of a deceased person's estate in accordance with his or her will?

A. Testamentary transfer
B. Intestate transfer
C. Inter-vivos transfer
D. Codicil transfer

19. Alex deposited $425 into a trust account at the end of each month for the past 4 years. The account is now worth $24,915. If interest was compounded monthly, what was the average annual compounded return over the 4-year period?

A. 6.8%
B. 7.2%
C. 8.4%
D. 9.9%

20. Which of the following is a fee charged to compensate an investment professional for buying and selling stocks and other securities?

A. Margin
B. Commission
C. Spread
D. Yield

21. Which of the following is/are correct regarding adverse selection?

(1) Individuals who are most likely to need insurance benefits are the ones least likely to purchase coverage.
(2) It occurs when high risk individuals are permitted to purchase insurance without paying adequate premiums for the risk assumed.

A. (1) only
B. (2) only
C. None of the above are correct.
D. All of the above are correct.

22. Which of the following consists of short-term promissory notes issued primarily by corporations that serve as a lower-cost alternative to bank loans?

A. Money market funds
B. Certificates of deposit
C. Commercial paper
D. Treasury bills

23. Which of the following involves investing money in equal portions, at regular intervals, regardless of fluctuations in the market?

A. Dollar cost averaging
B. Tactical asset allocation
C. Market timing
D. Value cost averaging

24. The two broad categories of qualified retirement plans are:

A. profit sharing and pension.
B. Roth and traditional.
C. SIMPLE and SEP.
D. defined contribution and defined benefit.

25. Which of the following forms of property ownership is only available for married couples?

A. Joint tenants with rights of survivorship
B. Tenancy in common
C. Tenancy by entirety
D. None of the above are correct.

26. Itemized deductions cannot be claimed by a taxpayer in the same year that he or she claims which of the following?

A. Personal exemption
B. Standard deduction
C. Personal allowance
D. Passive income

27. Which of the following serves as a guide in creating an investment program and involves determining the appropriate asset allocation, implementing the investment plan, and monitoring the results?

A. Form ADV
B. Investment policy statement
C. Preliminary prospectus
D. Summary prospectus

28. Which of the following is a type of managed care health insurance plan?

A. Comprehensive healthcare alliance
B. Integrated health advantage
C. Preferred provider organization
D. Optimal health network

29. A mutual fund that invests solely in technology stocks is an example of a:

A. domestic fund.
B. value fund.
C. hedge fund.
D. sector fund.

30. Which of the following are characteristics of group term life insurance?

(1) Relatively low cost to the employee.
(2) Requires a medical exam for employees to qualify for coverage.
(3) Possible loss of coverage if the employee terminates employment.
(4) Possible restrictions on the amount of coverage that may be obtained by the employee.

A. (1) and (4) only
B. (2) and (3) only
C. (1), (3), and (4) only
D. All of the above are correct.

31. Which of the following is a type of education tax credit?

A. American opportunity credit
B. Coverdell savings credit
C. 529 plan credit
D. Premium tax credit

32. The regulatory agency known as the SEC is the:

A. Select Examination Council.
B. Securities and Exchange Commission.
C. Securities Examination Commission.
D. Stock Exchange Council.

33. Andy made a $30,000 gift of a future interest to Robin. Assuming Andy is married, how much of the gift will qualify for the gift tax annual exclusion?

A. $0
B. $7,500
C. $15,000
D. $30,000

34. Which of the following are above-the-line deductions that may be claimed without a taxpayer itemizing deductions?

(1) Student loan interest
(2) Deductible traditional IRA contributions
(3) Ordinary and necessary business (Schedule C) expenses
(4) Health savings account contributions

A. (1) and (3) only
B. (1), (2), and (3) only
C. (2), (3), and (4) only
D. All of the above are correct.

35. All but which of the following are correct regarding the process of underwriting an insurance policy?

A. Underwriting refers to the process of selecting, classifying, and pricing applicants for insurance.
B. Restrictive underwriting typically results in higher overall claims made by policyholders.
C. The underwriter is the individual who decides to accept or reject an application, and under what conditions the policy may be issued.
D. One of the objectives of underwriting is to generate revenue while at the same time limiting the insurance company's assumed risk.

36. A 457 plan may be offered by which of the following?

A. Nonprofit organizations
B. Tax-exempt organizations
C. State, county, and local government agencies
D. All of the above are correct.

37. Long-term capital gains tax rates apply if an asset is held for:

A. longer than 6 months.
B. at least 6 months.
C. longer than 12 months.
D. at least 12 months.

38. All but which of the following are correct regarding Chapter 7 bankruptcy?

A. The debtor receives a discharge on all non-exempt dischargeable debts.
B. Chapter 7 is the most common form of bankruptcy filing.
C. The debtor must forfeit all assets.
D. All of the above are correct.

39. Which of the following risks is associated with complicated investment products, as well as investment products that charge a penalty for early withdrawal?

A. Liquidity risk
B. Sovereign risk
C. Event risk
D. Concentration risk

40. With a _______ power of attorney, the agent's ability to act on behalf of the principal comes into effect in the event of the principal's incapacity.

A. living
B. non-durable
C. springing
D. testamentary

41. If an insured selects a longer elimination period for a long-term care policy, the monthly ______ will be ______ than if a shorter elimination period is selected.

A. premium; higher
B. premium; lower
C. deductible; higher
D. deductible; lower

42. A premature distribution from a qualified plan, SEP, or IRA will incur a ______ penalty.

A. 5%
B. 10%
C. 15%
D. 20%

43. An adjustable-rate mortgage may be suitable in all but which of the following circumstances?

A. The borrower plans to own the home for only a few years.
B. The prevailing interest rate for a fixed-rate mortgage is too high.
C. The borrower expects a decrease in future earnings.
D. All of the above are correct.

44. All but which of the following are correct regarding a convertible bond?

A. It is a common stock that may be converted into a bond of the issuing corporation.
B. It may be converted at the bondholder's discretion.
C. It allows an investor to share in the growth of the corporation if the bond is converted into common stock.
D. Because of its flexibility, a convertible bond offers lower coupon rates than a non-convertible bond issued for the same term by the same issuer.

45. All but which of the following are correct regarding the role of a trustee?

A. If the trustee resigns, dies, or refuses to act as trustee, the trust still exists.
B. The trustee has a fiduciary duty to act at all times for the exclusive benefit of trust beneficiaries.
C. The trustee is legally responsible for the proper administration of the trust.
D. The trustee does not hold legal title to the trust property.

46. Which of the following is a formal examination of an individual's accounts and financial information to ensure information is reported correctly according to the tax laws and to verify the reported amount of tax is correct?

A. Authentication
B. Assessment
C. Audit
D. Accreditation

47. All but which of the following are characteristics of a universal life policy?

A. It is a form of permanent life insurance.
B. It has a flexible death benefit.
C. It has a minimum guaranteed cash value.
D. It has a flexible premium.

48. Which of the following is a tax-free transfer of a retirement plan participant's benefit from one retirement plan to another?

A. Conversion
B. Rollover
C. Lump sum distribution
D. Migration

49. Which of the following Acts prohibits creditors from discriminating against credit applicants on the basis of race, color, religion, national origin, sex, marital status, or age?

A. Truth in Lending Act (TILA)
B. Fair and Accurate Credit Transactions Act (FACTA)
C. Fair Credit Billing Act (FCBA)
D. Equal Credit Opportunity Act (ECOA)

50. All but which of the following are characteristics of exchange-traded funds (ETFs)?

A. They are traded on an exchange like individual securities.
B. Trades settle at the end of the trading day, similar to mutual funds.
C. They typically have lower expenses than mutual funds.
D. They are income tax efficient.

51. Which of the following estate planning goals can be accomplished through a will?

A. Establish a testamentary credit shelter trust.
B. Provide for decisions during incapacitation.
C. Avoid probate.
D. Provide burial wishes.

52. All but which of the following will lower an individual's tax liability?

A. Claiming fewer deductions.
B. Claiming more tax credits.
C. Claiming less income.
D. None of the above are correct.

53. When must an insurable interest exist for property insurance?

A. Only at the time the policy is written.
B. Only at the time the loss is claimed.
C. At the time the policy is written and at the time the loss is claimed.
D. An insurable interest is not required for property insurance.

The following information relates to questions 54 – 55.

Olivia, age 30, is an employee of Gamma Corporation. She participates in the company's 401(k) plan, which uses a 2 to 6-year graded vesting schedule. Olivia has been employed with the company for 4 full years.

54. What percentage of Olivia's salary deferrals are vested?

A. 40%
B. 60%
C. 80%
D. 100%

55. What percentage of the employer contributions in Olivia's 401(k) plan are vested?

A. 40%
B. 60%
C. 80%
D. 100%

56. Which of the following accounts allows individuals with disabilities to save money without losing their eligibility for federally funded benefits such as Medicaid or Supplemental Security Income (SSI)?

A. SAFE account
B. ABLE account
C. FLEX account
D. SECURE account

57. Which of the following is the risk associated with a particular company, industry, or sector?

A. Unsystematic risk
B. Systematic risk
C. Purchasing power risk
D. Market risk

58. Dennis establishes an irrevocable trust for the benefit of his two children and transfers $50,000 to the trustee of the trust. He gives his oldest child the right to lifetime income from the trust and, at the death of that child, the trust corpus will be distributed to the youngest child. Which of the following are correct regarding the transfer Dennis has made?

(1) The life estate of the first child qualifies for the gift tax annual exclusion because it is a future interest gift.
(2) The remainder interest of the second child does not qualify for the gift tax annual exclusion because it is a present interest gift.

A. (1) only
B. (2) only
C. None of the above are correct.
D. All of the above are correct.

59. Under the Social Security system, AIME is used to calculate which of the following?

A. PIA
B. APR
C. FICA
D. COLA

60. Which of the following is a legal claim against assets that are used as collateral to satisfy a debt?

A. Subrogation
B. Hypothecation
C. Pledge
D. Lien

61. Beth purchased a bond with a face value of $1,000 and a coupon rate of 4.5%. If the coupon payments are made semiannually, what is the periodic interest payment?

A. $16.88, paid twice per year.
B. $22.50, paid twice per year.
C. $45.00, paid once per year.
D. $45.00, paid twice per year.

62. Which of the following interests can be disclaimed by a beneficiary?

(1) A beneficiary's income interest in a revocable living trust.
(2) A beneficiary's right to the death benefit from a universal life insurance policy.
(3) A beneficiary's remainder interest in an irrevocable trust.
(4) A joint tenant's survivorship interest in an asset.

A. (1) and (3) only
B. (1) and (4) only
C. (2) and (3) only
D. All of the above are correct.

63. All but which of the following are correct regarding the cross-purchase form of a buy-sell agreement?

A. Each business owner purchases life insurance on the lives of the other business owners.
B. Life insurance proceeds provide surviving owners with money to buy the deceased owner's business interest from his or her estate.
C. If a company has three owners, then three life insurance policies will be purchased.
D. Each business owner pays the premiums for life insurance.

64. Target date funds are also known as:

A. sector funds.
B. industry funds.
C. lifecycle funds.
D. bond funds.

65. All but which of the following are correct regarding revolving credit?

A. Revolving credit is a type of installment debt.
B. It is a type of credit that does not have a fixed number of payments.
C. A credit card is an example of revolving credit.
D. If used responsibly, revolving credit can positively impact a borrower's credit score.

66. Which of the following behavioral finance concepts refers to the tendency for a person's feelings to influence and potentially distort his or her judgment and decision-making process?

A. Empathy gap
B. Motivated reasoning
C. Cognitive recognition
D. Emotional bias

67. In a personal automobile policy (PAP), which of the following losses would be considered "other-than-collision"?

(1) Flood
(2) Vandalism
(3) Falling objects
(4) Impact with a deer
(5) Impact with a large tree

A. (1), (3), and (5) only
B. (2), (4), and (5) only
C. (1), (2), (3), and (4) only
D. (2), (3), (4), and (5) only

68. Which of the following is/are correct regarding traditional IRAs?

(1) Spousal IRAs are available for non-working spouses.
(2) A husband and wife can open a joint IRA.

A. (1) only
B. (2) only
C. None of the above are correct.
D. All of the above are correct.

69. If the first month's interest payment on a loan is $612.50, and the interest rate is 7.5%, the mortgage balance is:

A. $97,000.
B. $98,000.
C. $99,000.
D. $100,000.

70. Which of the following is a measure of the length of time it takes for the price of a bond to be repaid through its internal cash flows?

A. Yield to maturity
B. Internal rate of return
C. Duration
D. Time weighted return

71. Which of the following is a legal document that changes a specific provision in a will?

A. Living will
B. Codicil
C. Power of appointment
D. Advance directive

72. A _______ is issued by a governmental body to finance a specific project. It is not backed by the full faith and credit of the issuing body. Instead, debts are repaid from revenue generated from the project that is being financed.

A. revenue bond
B. general obligation bond
C. private activity bond
D. multi-purpose bond

73. With a/an _____, the business owner has unlimited liability.

A. LLC
B. sole proprietorship
C. S corporation
D. C corporation

74. Joel made a lifetime gift of stock worth a total of $40,000 in equal shares to his two daughters. Joel's basis in the stock was $16,000. What is each daughter's basis in the stock they now own?

A. $8,000
B. $16,000
C. $20,000
D. $40,000

75. Which of the following steps of the financial planning process comes directly after analyzing the client's current course of action and potential alternate courses of action?

A. Developing the financial planning recommendations.
B. Implementing the financial planning recommendations.
C. Monitoring progress and updating.
D. Identifying and selecting goals.

ANSWER KEY

1. A
Megan would not owe any tax because the death benefit from a life insurance policy is not taxable income.

2. D
Treasury bills, commercial paper, and money market funds are cash equivalents.

3. C
Employee contributions to a defined contribution retirement plan are immediately vested.

4. D
The balance sheet is also referred to as the statement of financial position.

5. A
Leveraging involves using debt to increase an investment's expected return.

6. D
Gift tax is a tax on the transfer of property by one individual to another while receiving nothing, or less than full value, in return.

7. C
A reverse mortgage allows a homeowner to borrow money using his or her home as security for the loan. When a homeowner takes out a reverse mortgage, the title to the home remains in the borrower's name and the borrower does not make monthly mortgage payments.

8. C
In most states, if an insured commits suicide within the first two years after a life insurance policy is issued, the insurance company will pay only the cumulative premiums plus interest earned.

9. B
The type of investment known as a "REIT" is a real estate investment trust.

10. B
COBRA continuation coverage is provided to children of a covered employee due to the loss of dependent status because of age limitations or marriage. It must be identical to coverage provided to employees, apart from cost.

11. C
Money illusion is a type of cognitive error in behavioral finance that occurs when individuals view their wealth and income in nominal terms instead of inflation-adjusted terms.

12. B
TIPS (Treasury inflation-protected securities) are intended to protect investors against inflation risk.

13. B
Intestate succession is the legal process that determines the order of priority in which heirs would receive property if a decedent died without a valid will.

14. B
Donors can make irrevocable contributions of any amount into an UGMA or UTMA account, and the assets in the account become available to the minor when he or she reaches the age of the majority. UGMA and UTMA accounts are subject to kiddie tax rules.

15. D
Coinsurance is the percentage of costs of a covered health care service that an insured must pay (20%, for example) after having paid the deductible.

16. A
An employee's non-vested account balance will be forfeited if employment is terminated.

17. C
Modern portfolio theory is based on the assumption that investors are risk averse, and for a given level of risk investors prefer higher returns to lower returns.

18. A
A testamentary transfer is the distribution of a deceased person's estate in accordance with his or her will.

19. D
PMT = –$425
$n = 4 \times 12 = 48$
FV = $24,915
PV = 0
$i = ? = 0.8266 \times 12 = 9.9$

20. B
A commission is a fee charged to compensate an investment professional for buying and selling stocks and other securities.

21. B
Adverse selection occurs when high risk individuals are permitted to purchase insurance without paying adequate premiums for the risk assumed. Those individuals who are most likely to need insurance benefits are the ones most likely to purchase coverage.

22. C
Commercial paper consists of short-term promissory notes issued primarily by corporations that serve as a lower-cost alternative to bank loans.

23. A
Dollar cost averaging involves investing money in equal portions, at regular intervals, regardless of fluctuations in the market.

24. D
The two broad categories of qualified retirement plans are defined contribution and defined benefit.

25. C
Tenancy by entirety is a form of property ownership only available for married couples.

26. B
Itemized deductions cannot be claimed by a taxpayer in the same year that he or she claims the standard deduction.

27. B
An investment policy statement (IPS) serves as a guide in creating an investment program and involves determining the appropriate asset allocation, implementing the investment plan, and monitoring the results.

28. C
A preferred provider organization (PPO) is a type of managed care health insurance plan.

29. D
A mutual fund that invests solely in technology stocks is an example of a sector fund.

30. C
Group term life insurance has a relatively low cost to the employee, and there are possible restrictions on the amount of coverage that may be obtained. There is also a possible loss of coverage if the employee terminates employment. A medical exam is not required for an employee to qualify for group term life insurance coverage.

31. A
The American opportunity credit is a type of education tax credit.

32. B
The regulatory agency known as the SEC is the Securities and Exchange Commission.

33. A
Gifts of a future interest are not eligible for the gift tax annual exclusion.

34. D
Above-the-line deductions include student loan interest, deductible traditional IRA contributions, ordinary and necessary business (Schedule C) expenses, and health savings account contributions. These deductions may be claimed without a taxpayer itemizing deductions.

35. B
Underwriting refers to the process of selecting, classifying, and pricing applicants for insurance. The underwriter is the individual who decides to accept or reject an application, and under what conditions the policy may be issued. One of the objectives of underwriting is to generate revenue while at the same time limiting the insurance company's assumed risk. Restrictive underwriting typically results in lower overall claims made by policyholders.

36. D
A 457 plan may be offered by nonprofit organizations, tax-exempt organizations, and state, county, and local government agencies.

37. C
Long-term capital gains tax rates apply if an asset is held for longer than 12 months (at least 12 months and a day).

38. C
A debtor who files Chapter 7 bankruptcy may keep certain exempt assets, but all remaining assets will be forfeited. The debtor receives a discharge on all non-exempt dischargeable debts. Chapter 7 is the most common form of bankruptcy filing.

39. A
Liquidity risk is associated with complicated investment products, as well as investment products that charge a penalty for early withdrawal.

40. C
With a springing power of attorney, the agent's ability to act on behalf of the principal comes into effect in the event of the principal's incapacity.

41. B
If an insured selects a longer elimination period for a long-term care policy, the monthly premium will be lower than if a shorter elimination period is selected.

42. B
A premature distribution from a qualified plan, SEP, or IRA will incur a 10% penalty.

43. C
An adjustable-rate mortgage may be suitable if the borrower plans to own the home for only a few years, if the prevailing interest rate for a fixed-rate mortgage is too high, or if the borrower expects an increase in future earnings.

44. A
A convertible bond is a bond that may be converted into the common stock of the issuing corporation. It may be converted at the bondholder's discretion, and it allows an investor to share in the growth of the corporation if the bond is converted into common stock. Because of its flexibility, a convertible bond offers lower coupon rates than a non-convertible bond issued for the same term by the same issuer.

45. D
The trustee holds legal title to the trust property and is legally responsible for the proper administration of the trust. The trustee has a fiduciary duty to act at all times for the exclusive benefit of trust beneficiaries. If the trustee resigns, dies, or refuses to act as trustee, the trust still exists.

46. C
An audit is a formal examination of an individual's accounts and financial information to ensure information is reported correctly according to the tax laws and to verify the reported amount of tax is correct.

47. C
A universal life policy is a form of permanent life insurance with a flexible death benefit and a flexible premium. It does not have a minimum guaranteed cash value.

48. B
A rollover is a tax-free transfer of a retirement plan participant's benefit from one retirement plan to another.

49. D
The Equal Credit Opportunity Act (ECOA) prohibits creditors from discriminating against credit applicants on the basis of race, color, religion, national origin, sex, marital status, or age.

50. B
ETFs are traded on an exchange and may be bought or sold throughout the trading day like individual securities. They typically have lower expenses than mutual funds and are income tax efficient.

51. A
Wills do not avoid probate. Planning for incapacity is addressed through powers of attorney, not through the will. The will is often read after the decedent's funeral, so burial wishes should not be included in the will. A will can be used to establish a testamentary credit shelter trust.

52. A
Claiming more tax credits and less income will lower an individual's tax liability. Claiming fewer deductions will raise an individual's tax liability.

53. C
For property insurance, an insurable interest must exist at the time the policy is written and at the time the loss is claimed.

54. D
Employee salary deferrals are always fully vested.

55. B
Vested employer contributions = 3 years × 20% per year = 60%

56. B
An ABLE account allows individuals with disabilities to save money without losing their eligibility for federally funded benefits such as Medicaid or Supplemental Security Income (SSI).

57. A
Unsystematic risk is the risk associated with a particular company, industry, or sector.

58. C
The life estate of the first child qualifies for the gift tax annual exclusion because it is a present interest gift. The remainder interest of the second child does not qualify for the gift tax annual exclusion because it is a future interest gift.

59. A
Under the Social Security system, AIME (average indexed monthly earnings) is used to calculate PIA (primary insurance amount).

60. D
A lien is a legal claim against assets that are used as collateral to satisfy a debt.

61. B
Periodic interest payment = (\$1,000 × 0.045) / 2 = \$22.50

62. D
All the interests listed may be disclaimed by filing a qualified disclaimer.

63. C
With the cross-purchase form of a buy-sell agreement, each business owner purchases life insurance on the lives of the other business owners, and each business owner pays the premiums for life insurance. The life insurance proceeds provide the surviving owners with money to buy the deceased owner's business interest from his or her estate. If a company has three owners, then six life insurance policies will be purchased.

64. C
Target date funds are also known as lifecycle funds.

65. A
Revolving credit is a type of credit that does not have a fixed number of payments. A credit card is an example of revolving credit. If used responsibly, it can positively impact a borrower's credit score. Revolving credit is not a type of installment debt.

66. D
Emotional bias is the behavioral finance concept that refers to the tendency for a person's feelings to influence and potentially distort his or her judgment and decision-making process.

67. C
Other-than-collision coverage will pay for losses that result from flood, vandalism, falling objects, and impact with an animal. Impact with a tree is considered collision.

68. A
Spousal IRAs are available for non-working spouses. Joint IRAs are not permitted.

69. B
Step 1: Monthly interest rate = 0.075 / 12 months = 0.00625
Step 2: Mortgage balance = \$612.50 / 0.00625 = \$98,000

70. C
Duration is a measure of the length of time it takes for the price of a bond to be repaid through its internal cash flows.

71. B
A codicil is a legal document that changes a specific provision in a will.

72. A
A revenue bond is issued by a governmental body to finance a specific project. It is not backed by the full faith and credit of the issuing body. Instead, debts are repaid from revenue generated from the project that is being financed.

73. B
With a sole proprietorship, the business owner has unlimited liability.

74. A
There is no step-up in basis for lifetime gifts. $16,000 / 2 daughters = $8,000 basis for each daughter.

75. A
After analyzing the client's current course of action and potential alternate courses of action, the next step of the financial planning process is developing the financial planning recommendations.

PRACTICE EXAM 4

QUESTIONS

1. All but which of the following are correct regarding a mutual fund's turnover rate?

A. A mutual fund with a high turnover rate will generally require more active management and will charge higher expenses.
B. The higher the turnover rate, the more tax efficient the mutual fund will be.
C. A mutual fund with a high turnover rate is best positioned in a tax-deferred account.
D. All of the above are correct.

2. Which of the following is/are correct regarding probate?

(1) A decedent's estate will pay more federal estate tax if assets pass through probate.
(2) Probate is held only in the state where the decedent dies.

A. (1) only
B. (2) only
C. None of the above are correct.
D. All of the above are correct.

3. Which of the following is the general upward price movement of goods and services in an economy?

A. Disinflation
B. Stagflation
C. Reflation
D. Inflation

4. Which of the following states that all relevant information is fully and immediately reflected in a security's market price, thereby assuming that an investor will obtain an equilibrium rate of return?

A. Modern portfolio theory
B. Random walk theory
C. Efficient market hypothesis
D. Capital asset pricing model

5. Which of the following is the starting point for calculating a decedent's federal estate tax?

A. Gross estate
B. Adjusted estate
C. Net estate
D. Tentative estate

6. A doctor starting a new medical practice is concerned about limiting her personal liability. She would like to have flow-through taxation and the ability to easily sell partial ownership interest in her practice in the future. Which of the following entities is most suitable for the doctor to meet her goals?

A. S corporation
B. C corporation
C. Sole proprietorship
D. Limited partnership

7. All but which of the following are correct regarding term life insurance?

A. There is no cash value accumulation in a term policy.
B. Loans may be permitted.
C. Term life insurance is often less expensive than whole life insurance on a per premium dollar basis.
D. All of the above are correct.

8. Which of the following allows employees who have lost their jobs to continue receiving identical health coverage that was provided through their group health insurance plan?

A. Medicare Advantage
B. Health savings account
C. Affordable Care Act
D. COBRA

9. Which of the following is a defined contribution plan that uses a fixed percentage of compensation formula to determine required annual contributions to employee accounts?

A. Money purchase plan
B. Profit sharing plan
C. Defined benefit plan
D. None of the above are correct.

10. Which of the following is correct regarding a bond's coupon rate?

A. It is always equal to its yield to maturity.
B. It is the stated annual interest rate that will be paid each year for the term of a bond.
C. It is stated as a percentage of the current market price of a bond.
D. A 5% coupon bond will pay $50 each semiannual period for a $1,000 bond.

11. All but which of the following are correct regarding an IPO?

A. It provides an opportunity for investors to own and participate in the growth of a formerly private company.
B. An IPO can be a risky and speculative investment.
C. An IPO helps establish a trading market for shares of stock.
D. All of the above are correct.

12. Which of the following is a type of permanent life insurance that insures the lives of two people, usually spouses?

A. Variable universal life insurance
B. Participating whole life insurance
C. Survivorship whole life insurance
D. Modified endowment contract

13. Dan owns a house that he would like to pass to his grandchild at death. Instead of waiting, he gives his grandchild the house today with the provision that he can continue to live in it for the rest of his life. Which of the following interests has Dan given?

A. A remainder interest
B. A reversionary interest
C. A term interest
D. A life estate interest

14. Reframing and explaining are forms of ______ between an advisor and client.

A. directive counseling skills
B. nondirective counseling skills
C. cognitive errors
D. emotional biases

15. Relating to the time value of money, a/an ______ is when a payment is made at the beginning of the period.

A. serial annuity
B. annuity due
C. present value annuity
D. future value annuity

16. All but which of the following are types of Treasury investments?

A. Treasury bills
B. Treasury notes
C. Treasury stocks
D. Treasury bonds

17. When the gift splitting election is made, gifts made by either spouse are treated as being made ______ by each spouse.

A. 0%
B. 50%
C. 75%
D. 100%

18. A prenuptial agreement is intended to address which of the following issues?

A. Who will own assets brought to a marriage.
B. Who will be responsible for child support payments.
C. Who will receive custody of children born during marriage.
D. Who will pay alimony and in what amount.

19. Which of the following methods are commonly used to value an insured's home and property for purposes of providing reimbursement for damage after a covered loss?

A. Appraised cash value and replacement cost value
B. Actual cash value and risk adjusted value
C. Dwelling value and risk adjusted value
D. Actual cash value and replacement cost value

20. All but which of the following are characteristics of a SEP IRA?

A. A SEP IRA is 100% owned by the participant.
B. A SEP IRA is fully vested at all times.
C. Plan loans are permitted.
D. All of the above are correct.

21. An advisor can satisfy the "brochure rule" by providing the client with which of the following?

A. Form ADV, Part 1
B. Form ADV, Part 2
C. Prospectus
D. Addendum

22. All but which of the following are correct regarding a mutual fund sales load?

A. Not every type of shareholder fee is a sales load.
B. A no-load fund may charge fees that are not sales loads.
C. No-load funds do not charge operating expenses.
D. All of the above are correct.

23. All but which of the following are forms of property ownership?

A. Joint proprietorship
B. Tenancy by entirety
C. Tenancy in common
D. Community property

24. Which of the following limits is imposed on direct charitable contributions made at death?

A. Direct charitable contributions are limited to 10% of the decedent's gross estate.
B. Direct charitable contributions are limited to 50% of the decedent's gross estate.
C. Direct charitable contributions are limited to 75% of the decedent's gross estate.
D. Direct charitable contributions can be made at death without limit.

For questions 25 – 28, match the method of risk management with the description that follows. Use only one answer per blank. Answers may be used more than once or not at all.

A. Retention
B. Transfer
C. Reduction
D. Avoidance

25. ____ If a loss occurs, it will be absorbed.

26. ____ Effectively making changes so a loss cannot occur.

27. ____ When a loss is large enough that it cannot be retained, insurance is purchased.

28. ____ An attempt to reduce the chance that a loss will occur.

29. In a SWOT analysis, the "T" stands for:

A. threats.
B. trends.
C. traps.
D. terms.

30. Which of the following typically invest in high-quality, short-term investments such as Treasury bills, commercial paper, and negotiable CDs? The underlying investments have an average maturity of 30 to 90 days.

A. Treasury notes
B. Commercial paper
C. Money market funds
D. Certificates of deposit

31. William would like to set up a revocable living trust but is concerned about potential adverse tax consequences. If he sets up a revocable living trust and places all of his income producing assets into the trust, how will the income from the trust be taxed?

A. The income will be taxed at trust tax rates.
B. The income will pass through to William, who will pay it personally.
C. The income will accumulate tax-free within the trust.
D. Part of the income will pass through to William, who will pay it personally, and part of the income will accumulate tax-free within the trust.

32. Lucy will take a $30,000 distribution from her 401(k) plan before the end of the year to purchase a new car. She is 58 years old and recently retired from her job. Assuming that she is in the 25% tax bracket, she will have to pay a ______ premature distribution penalty.

A. $0
B. $3,000
C. $6,000
D. $7,500

33. All but which of the following are types of tax credits?

A. Earned income credit
B. Foreign tax credit
C. Lifetime learning credit
D. Business advancement credit

34. Which of the following is a measure of the cash flow an investor receives on the money invested in a security?

A. Retained earnings
B. Surplus
C. Yield
D. Profit

35. Which of the following is the correct formula used to calculate the amount of each annual variable annuity payment that can be excluded from an annuitant's ordinary income?

A. Exclusion ratio = number of years of expected return / investment in contract
B. Exclusion ratio = investment in contract / number of years of expected return
C. Exclusion ratio = 1 – (number of years of return / investment in contract)
D. Exclusion ratio = 1 – (investment in contract / number of years of return)

36. Which of the following is/are correct regarding ERISA?

(1) ERISA establishes criteria for investment selection for qualified retirement plans.
(2) ERISA establishes minimum funding, eligibility, coverage, and vesting requirements for qualified retirement plans.

A. (1) only
B. (2) only
C. None of the above are correct.
D. All of the above are correct.

37. Exchange rate risk is a type of:

A. systematic risk.
B. unsystematic risk.
C. tax risk.
D. political risk.

38. Jerry and Katie Smith have lived in a community property state all their married lives. They own a house that is registered only in Katie's name. If she dies, what will happen to the house?

A. The house will pass automatically to Jerry.
B. The house will pass automatically to Katie's closest family member.
C. The house will pass through Katie's will, and the entire house will go to Jerry.
D. Katie's half will pass by will. Jerry already owns half under community property laws.

39. Which of the following is a type of emotional bias in behavioral finance that refers to an individual's tendency to put his or her short-term needs ahead of long-term goals?

A. Conservatism bias
B. Self-control bias
C. Affinity bias
D. Status quo bias

40. Which of the following is the maximum exclusion of gain on the sale of a principal residence for a single taxpayer who owned the house and used it as a principal residence during at least 2 of the last 5 years before the date of sale?

A. $0
B. $125,000
C. $250,000
D. $500,000

41. Insurance companies are classified as either _______ or _______ depending on their organizational structure.

A. participating; mutual
B. regulated; unregulated
C. qualified; nonqualified
D. mutual; stock

42. Kyle, age 35, has been a plan participant in his employer's SIMPLE IRA for one year. If he makes a withdrawal of $8,000 this year, he will be subject to which of the following early withdrawal penalties?

A. $0
B. $800
C. $2,000
D. $4,000

43. Which of the following trusts does not qualify for the unlimited marital deduction in the grantor's estate, and trust assets are not included in the gross estate of the surviving spouse?

A. Credit shelter trust
B. Marital trust
C. QTIP trust
D. Estate trust

44. Housing debt costs, including principal, interest, taxes, and insurance, should not exceed _______ of gross income.

A. 15%
B. 20%
C. 28%
D. 36%

45. Which of the following is correct regarding financial risk?

A. Financial risk is a type of non-diversifiable risk.
B. Companies that issue debt have a higher degree of financial risk than companies financed by equity.
C. Financial risk is the same as business risk.
D. All of the above are correct.

46. Which of the following is a tax imposed on a specific good or transaction? Examples include the tax on gasoline and alcoholic beverages.

A. Capital gain tax
B. Excise tax
C. Wealth tax
D. Progressive tax

47. Which of the following is a type of insurance coverage purchased by a professional who can cause financial harm to another person?

A. Errors and omissions insurance
B. Umbrella insurance
C. Malpractice insurance
D. None of the above are correct.

48. Which of the following groups may be eligible to participate in a 403(b) plan?

A. Public school employees
B. Not-for-profit hospital employees
C. Church employees
D. All of the above are correct.

49. Which of the following is/are correct regarding interest paid from municipal bonds?

(1) Interest paid from municipal bonds is not taxed by the federal government.
(2) Interest paid from municipal bonds is never taxable at the state level.

A. (1) only
B. (2) only
C. None of the above are correct.
D. All of the above are correct.

50. If a trust is created and funded with $100,000, that money is the:

A. testate.
B. devise.
C. corpus.
D. bequest.

51. On which of the following financial statements would retirement account values be provided?

A. Cash flow statement
B. Budget
C. Income statement
D. Statement of financial position

52. A mutual fund that invests in securities both inside and outside the U.S. is known as a/an:

A. long-short fund.
B. global fund.
C. international fund.
D. balanced fund.

53. All but which of the following can refer to the person appointed by a court who is responsible for carrying out the provisions of a decedent's will?

A. Executor
B. Personal representative
C. Estate ward
D. Estate administrator

54. The three main classifications of income are:

A. earned, passive, and portfolio.
B. material, passive, and portfolio.
C. earned, passive, and capital.
D. passive, portfolio, and material.

55. All but which of the following are correct regarding group disability coverage?

A. The coverage remains in effect until employment is terminated.
B. Evidence of insurability is not required to qualify for coverage.
C. It provides a disabled employee with an annual benefit typically up to 100% of his or her pre-disability income.
D. All of the above are correct.

56. In which of the following retirement plans does an employee pay a portion of his or her base salary into the plan?

A. Non-depository retirement plan
B. Depository retirement plan
C. Non-contributory retirement plan
D. Contributory retirement plan

57. Which of the following is correct regarding the difference between a 15-year mortgage and a 30-year mortgage?

A. A 30-year mortgage will allow for a more affordable monthly payment.
B. A 15-year mortgage will charge more interest over the life of the loan.
C. A 15-year mortgage is commonly known as a "reverse" mortgage.
D. None of the above are correct.

58. Which of the following is correct in the event of corporate bankruptcy?

A. Common stockholders receive funds before preferred stockholders.
B. Preferred stockholders receive funds before common stockholders.
C. Common stockholders and preferred stockholders receive funds at the same time.
D. Neither common stockholders nor preferred stockholders are eligible to receive funds.

59. A living will has which of the following characteristics?

A. It allows an individual to appoint property before death.
B. It allows an individual to specify wishes about medical treatment and artificial life support under certain circumstances.
C. It has the same function as a revocable living trust.
D. All of the above are correct.

60. Which of the following is correct regarding a FICO score?

A. A high FICO score will generally result in a lower interest rate offered on new debt.
B. A high FICO score will generally result in a higher interest rate offered on new debt.
C. A FICO score is not correlated to the interest rate offered on new debt.
D. None of the above are correct.

61. Which of the following is a tax credit for workers with low to moderate income? Eligibility for the credit is based on various factors including family size, filing status, and income.

A. Itemized deduction credit
B. Standard deduction credit
C. Earned income credit
D. Municipal income credit

62. Which of the following is a type of managed care health insurance plan?

A. Preferred managed care provider
B. Total managed care provider
C. Preferred maintenance plan
D. Health maintenance organization

63. Which of the following is a bond's rate of return if interest payments are reinvested at an equal rate and the bond is held to maturity?

A. Current yield
B. Nominal yield
C. Yield to maturity
D. Duration

64. The account known as an "ESOP" is an:

A. employer stock option plan.
B. employee stock ownership plan.
C. employee simplified ownership pension.
D. employee strategic ownership program.

65. To establish a Coverdell education savings account, the beneficiary must be under age _______ unless the individual is designated as a special needs beneficiary, and money in the account must be used by the time the beneficiary is _______ years of age.

A. 14; 25
B. 18; 30
C. 21; 35
D. 25; 40

66. Which of the following type of REIT participates in the acquisition, management, renovation, and sale of real estate and generates income through capital gains and rental income?

A. Hybrid REIT
B. Mortgage REIT
C. Equity REIT
D. Commercial REIT

67. Which of the following correctly describes a qualified retirement plan participant's "normal retirement age"?

A. It is considered to be age 59 ½ regardless of when the plan participant was born.
B. It is considered to be age 65 regardless of when the plan participant was born.
C. It is the age at which a plan participant is eligible to leave the workforce and start receiving partial retirement benefits.
D. It is the age at which a plan participant is eligible to leave the workforce and start receiving full retirement benefits.

68. Greg sued his former employer and won a judgment that provides him $2,000 at the end of each 6-month period for the next 5 years. If the account that holds Greg's settlement earns an average annual rate of 7% compounded semiannually, how much was the employer initially required to pay Greg?

A. $15,328.29
B. $16,633.21
C. $17,215.37
D. $18,108.38

69. Which of the following explains why an individual wants to achieve certain financial goals and is subjective in nature?

A. Analytical data
B. Systematic data
C. Quantitative data
D. Qualitative data

70. Which of the following is an absolute measure of the investment performance of a diversified portfolio?

A. Alpha
B. Beta
C. Yield
D. Sharpe

71. Which of the following is/are correct regarding the generation-skipping transfer tax (GSTT)?

(1) A transferor's spouse or former spouse, regardless of age, is not a skip person for GSTT purposes.
(2) The generation-skipping transfer tax is commonly imposed on transfers from grandparents to grandchildren or great-grandchildren.

A. (1) only
B. (2) only
C. None of the above are correct.
D. All of the above are correct.

72. ______ can bind coverage because they work for the insurer; ______ cannot bind coverage.

A. Brokers; agents
B. Advisors; brokers
C. Agents; brokers
D. Brokers; advisors

73. When calculating Social Security benefits, "AIME" stands for which of the following?

A. Average indexed monthly earnings
B. Average income marginal earnings
C. Annual indexed monthly estimate
D. Annual income marginal estimate

74. Chris and Sarah were married when Chris died unexpectedly in May of the current year. They had no dependents. Which of the following is Sarah's tax filing status for the current year?

A. Single
B. Head of household
C. Married filing jointly
D. Domestic partner

75. A cash balance plan is a ______ plan with features similar to a ______ plan.

A. defined benefit; defined contribution
B. defined contribution; defined benefit
C. pension; profit sharing
D. profit sharing; pension

ANSWER KEY

1. B
A mutual fund with a high turnover rate will generally require more active management and will charge higher expenses. The higher the turnover rate, the less tax efficient the mutual fund will be. A mutual fund with a high turnover rate is best positioned in a tax-deferred account.

2. C
The federal estate tax is not affected by probate, although administrative costs may be reduced if probate is avoided. Probate may be held in a state other than where the decedent died. This is known as ancillary probate.

3. D
Inflation is the general upward price movement of goods and services in an economy.

4. C
The efficient market hypothesis states that all relevant information is fully and immediately reflected in a security's market price, thereby assuming that an investor will obtain an equilibrium rate of return.

5. A
The gross estate is the starting point for calculating a decedent's federal estate tax.

6. A
A C corporation would not provide flow-through taxation as the doctor requested. A sole proprietorship would not limit her liability. A limited partnership may be appropriate, but there is no mention of a general partner. The best answer is the S corporation.

7. B
Loans from term life insurance policies are not permitted because there is no cash value accumulation. Term life insurance is often less expensive than whole life insurance on a per premium dollar basis.

8. D
COBRA allows employees who have lost their jobs to continue receiving identical health coverage that was provided through their group health insurance plan.

9. A
A money purchase plan is a defined contribution plan that uses a fixed percentage of compensation formula to determine required annual contributions to employee accounts.

10. B
A bond's coupon rate is the stated annual interest rate that will be paid each year for the term of a bond. It is stated as a percentage of the bond's face value. A 5% coupon bond will pay $50 per year, not per semiannual period.

11. D
An IPO (initial public offering) provides an opportunity for investors to own and participate in the growth of a formerly private company. It helps establish a trading market for shares of stock and can be a risky and speculative investment.

12. C
Survivorship whole life insurance is a type of permanent life insurance that insures the lives of two people, usually spouses.

13. A
Dan has given his grandchild a remainder interest in the house. He did not give a reversionary interest because the house does not return to Dan. A term interest would be for a limited time only, but the question states "for the rest of his life." A life estate would give Dan a controlling interest for his life, which he does not have.

14. A
Reframing and explaining are forms of directive counseling skills between an advisor and client.

15. B
Relating to the time value of money, an annuity due is when a payment is made at the beginning of the period.

16. C
Treasury bills, Treasury notes, and Treasury bonds are types of Treasury investments.

17. B
When the gift splitting election is made, gifts made by either spouse are treated as being made 50% by each spouse.

18. A
A prenuptial agreement is intended to address who will own assets brought to a marriage.

19. D
Actual cash value and replacement cost value are commonly used to value an insured's home and property for the purposes of providing reimbursement for damage after a covered loss.

20. C
A SEP IRA is 100% owned by the participant and is fully vested at all times. Plan loans are not permitted from SEP IRAs.

21. B
To satisfy the brochure rule, the advisor can provide the client with Form ADV, Part 2, or the advisor can provide an actual brochure that contains the same information that would be found in Form ADV, Part 2.

22. C
Not every type of shareholder fee is a sales load. A no-load fund may charge fees that are not sales loads, such as operating expenses.

23. A
Tenancy by entirety, tenancy in common, and community property are forms of property ownership.

24. D
Direct charitable contributions can be made at death without limit.

25. A
By retaining risk, if a loss occurs it will be absorbed.

26. D
Avoidance is effectively making changes so a loss cannot occur.

27. B
When a loss is large enough that it cannot be retained, the risk is transferred to an insurance company.

28. C
Reduction is an attempt to reduce the chance that a loss will occur.

29. A
In a SWOT analysis, the "T" stands for threats.

30. C
Money market funds typically invest in high-quality, short-term investments, such as Treasury bills, commercial paper, and negotiable CDs. The underlying investments have an average maturity of 30 to 90 days.

31. B
Because this is a revocable living trust, the income will pass through to William, who will pay it personally. The trust itself is tax neutral.

32. A
Distributions from a 401(k) plan following separation from service after reaching age 55 are not subject to the 10% premature distribution penalty. The question asks about the premature distribution penalty that Lucy will pay, not the taxes that she will owe on the distribution.

33. D
The earned income credit, foreign tax credit, and lifetime learning credit are types of tax credits.

34. C
Yield is a measure of the cash flow an investor receives on the money invested in a security.

35. B
Exclusion ratio = investment in contract / number of years of expected return

36. B
ERISA establishes minimum funding, eligibility, coverage, and vesting requirements for qualified retirement plans.

37. A
Exchange rate risk is a type of systematic risk.

38. D
Unless the house was bought by Katie with money earned prior to marriage, or with gift or inheritance money, the house is community property. The question does not provide this information, and it cannot be assumed. Therefore, Katie's half of the house will pass by will. Jerry already owns half of the house under community property laws.

39. B
Self-control bias is a type of emotional bias in behavioral finance that refers to an individual's tendency to put his or her short-term needs ahead of long-term goals.

40. C
The maximum exclusion of gain on the sale of a principal residence for a single taxpayer who owned the house and used it as a principal residence during at least 2 of the last 5 years before the date of sale is $250,000.

41. D
Insurance companies are classified as either mutual or stock depending on their organizational structure.

42. C
$8,000 × 25% = $2,000
Early withdrawals from a SIMPLE IRA are subject to a 25% penalty if the withdrawals are made during the first two years of plan participation. After the initial two-year period, the early withdrawal penalty is reduced to 10%.

43. A
A credit shelter trust (B trust) does not qualify for the unlimited marital deduction in the grantor's estate. The trust assets are not included in the gross estate of the surviving spouse.

44. C
Housing debt costs, including principal, interest, taxes, and insurance, should not exceed 28% of gross income.

45. B
Companies that issue debt have a higher degree of financial risk than companies financed by equity.

46. B
Excise tax is a tax imposed on a specific good or transaction. Examples include the tax on gasoline and alcoholic beverages.

47. A
Errors and omissions insurance is a type of insurance coverage purchased by a professional who can cause financial harm to another person.

48. D
403(b) plan participants may include public school employees, not-for-profit hospital employees, and church employees.

49. A
Interest paid from municipal bonds is not taxed by the federal government. The bond interest may also be tax-exempt by various states if certain requirements are met.

50. C
If a trust is created and funded with $100,000, that money is the corpus.

51. D
Retirement account values are provided on the statement of financial position.

52. B
A mutual fund that invests in securities both inside and outside the U.S. is known as a global fund.

53. C
The person appointed by a court who is responsible for carrying out the provisions of a decedent's will is the executor. Other terms for executor include personal representative and estate administrator.

54. A
The three main classifications of income are earned, passive, and portfolio.

55. C
Group disability coverage provides a disabled employee with an annual benefit typically up to 70% of his or her pre-disability income. The coverage remains in effect until employment is terminated, and evidence of insurability is not required.

56. D
With a contributory retirement plan, an employee pays a portion of his or her base salary into the plan.

57. A
A 15-year mortgage will charge less interest over the life of the loan compared to a 30-year mortgage, but the 30-year mortgage will allow for a more affordable monthly payment.

58. B
Preferred stockholders receive funds before common stockholders in the event of corporate bankruptcy.

59. B
A living will is a legal document in which an individual specifies what type of medical treatment he or she prefers in the event of an emergency. Specifically, it addresses the individual's wishes about artificial life support. A living will is also known as an advance medical directive.

60. A
A high FICO score will generally result in a lower interest rate offered on new debt.

61. C
The earned income credit is a tax credit for workers with low to moderate income. Eligibility is based on various factors including family size, filing status, and income.

62. D
A health maintenance organization (HMO) is a type of managed care health insurance plan.

63. C
A bond's yield to maturity is its rate of return if interest payments are reinvested at an equal rate and the bond is held to maturity.

64. B
The account known as an "ESOP" is an employee stock ownership plan.

65. B
To establish a Coverdell education savings account, the beneficiary must be under age 18 unless the individual is designated as a special needs beneficiary, and money in the account must be used by the time the beneficiary is 30 years of age.

66. C
An equity REIT participates in the acquisition, management, renovation, and sale of real estate and generates income through capital gains and rental income.

67. D
A qualified retirement plan participant's "normal retirement age" is the age at which a plan participant is eligible to leave the workforce and start receiving full retirement benefits.

68. B
PMT = –$2,000
n = 5 × 2 = 10
i = 7 / 2 = 3.5
FV = 0
PV = ? = $16,633.21

69. D
Qualitative data explains why an individual wants to achieve certain financial goals and is subjective in nature.

70. A
Alpha (Jensen's alpha) is an absolute measure of the investment performance of a diversified portfolio.

71. D
A transferor's spouse or former spouse, regardless of age, is not a skip person for GSTT purposes. The generation-skipping transfer tax is commonly imposed on transfers from grandparents to grandchildren or great-grandchildren.

72. C
Agents can bind coverage because they work for the insurer; brokers cannot bind coverage.

73. A
When calculating Social Security benefits, "AIME" is the average indexed monthly earnings.

74. C
Sarah's tax filing status for the current year is married filing jointly. A taxpayer whose spouse died during the tax year is considered married for the entire year. The surviving spouse is eligible to file as married filing jointly.

75. A
A cash balance plan is a defined benefit plan with features similar to a defined contribution plan.

PRACTICE EXAM 5

QUESTIONS

1. Which of the following is the risk that a bond issuer will default?

A. Market risk
B. Credit risk
C. Tax risk
D. Interest rate risk

2. With the _______ form of property ownership, two or more individuals share ownership of a property, and the ownership shares may be unequal.

A. tenancy in common
B. joint tenants with rights of survivorship
C. tenancy by entirety
D. community property

3. Which of the following refers to the decrease in the amount of certain tax credits above a specific income level?

A. Depreciation
B. Amortization
C. Elimination
D. Phaseout

4. If the gift tax annual exclusion is $18,000, which of the following is correct?

A. An individual can gift an unlimited amount of present interest gifts to up to 10 recipients without incurring a federal gift tax.
B. An individual can gift an unlimited amount of future interest gifts to an unlimited number of recipients without incurring a federal gift tax.
C. An individual can gift up to $18,000 of future interest gifts to up to 10 recipients without incurring a federal gift tax.
D. An individual can gift up to $18,000 of present interest gifts to an unlimited number of recipients without incurring a federal gift tax.

5. Which of the following is/are correct regarding profit sharing plans?

(1) Profit sharing plans are a type of defined contribution pension plan.
(2) The minimum funding standard requires that employers make annual contributions.

A. (1) only
B. (2) only
C. None of the above are correct.
D. All of the above are correct.

6. All but which of the following are correct regarding Chapter 13 bankruptcy?

A. It is referred to as "individual debt adjustment" or the "wage earner's plan."
B. A debtor proposes a repayment plan to make installment payments to creditors over a period of time.
C. A debtor may not use Chapter 13 bankruptcy proceedings to avoid home foreclosure.
D. All of the above are correct.

7. Which of the following is designed to provide mutual fund investors with key fund information in a clear and concise format?

A. Indenture agreement
B. Debenture agreement
C. Summary prospectus
D. Form ADV

8. Which of the following is the concept that if an injured party was partially responsible for causing an accident, he or she will be denied compensation for damages?

A. Contributory negligence
B. Comparative negligence
C. Subrogation
D. Morale hazard

9. Which of the following is the tax filing deadline for the majority of taxpayers in the U.S.?

A. January 1st
B. April 15th
C. July 15th
D. December 31st

10. Which of the following analyzes and assesses the risks associated with providing insurance to individuals and establishes the pricing of insurance premiums?

A. Adjuster
B. Agent
C. Broker
D. Underwriter

11. Which of the following replaces a percentage of a worker's pre-retirement income based on his or her lifetime earnings?

A. Social Security
B. Social Welfare
C. Medicare
D. Medicaid

12. Which of the following will result if the periodic payments made on a loan are not enough to pay the amount of interest that accrues on the loan's principal?

A. Amortization
B. Negative amortization
C. Depreciation
D. Negative depreciation

13. Which of the following are two common forms of analysis used by investors to evaluate markets and securities?

A. General analysis and specific analysis
B. Broad analysis and specialized analysis
C. Technical analysis and fundamental analysis
D. Alpha analysis and beta analysis

14. Gifts made during a donor's lifetime receive a _______ of basis, and gifts made at death receive a _______ of basis.

A. carryover; step-up
B. step-up; carryover
C. carryover; carryover
D. step-up; step-up

15. Exaggerating a loss to an insurance company to collect a larger benefit payment is considered a _______ hazard.

A. morale
B. moral
C. physical
D. negligent

16. Which of the following is correct regarding traditional IRAs?

A. Loans are permitted for a first-time home purchase.
B. Loans are permitted for qualified medical expenses.
C. Loans are permitted for qualified education expenses.
D. Loans are not permitted.

17. All but which of the following occurs when an investor buys a corporate bond?

A. The investor borrows money from the company issuing the bond.
B. The company issuing the bond commits to paying interest to the investor.
C. The company issuing the bond commits to returning the principal to the investor when the bond matures.
D. All of the above are correct.

18. Elle has a mortgage with a current balance of $613,564. The monthly payment is $3,849, and her house was appraised for $902,300. What is the loan-to-value ratio?

A. 62%
B. 64%
C. 66%
D. 68%

19. Which of the following is the correct rationale for purchasing an investment in a portfolio?

A. Growth stocks because they pay high dividends.
B. FNMA securities because they are backed by the full faith and credit of the U.S. government.
C. A REIT because it provides exposure to real estate.
D. A global fund because it provides only international exposure.

20. Which of the following is a tax on the transfer of assets to a person two or more generations younger than the donor?

A. Generation-skipping transfer tax
B. Inheritance transfer tax
C. Testamentary transfer tax
D. Family wealth transfer tax

21. Child support payments are ______ to the payor and ______ to the recipient.

A. deductible; taxable
B. non-deductible; tax-free
C. taxable; deductible
D. tax-free; non-deductible

22. A small business owner who maintains a retail store in a high-risk neighborhood installs shatterproof windows and a security system to prevent theft. Which method of risk management is the store owner using?

A. Avoidance
B. Diversification
C. Reduction
D. Transfer

23. All but which of the following are correct regarding a Pell grant?

A. It is an education grant distributed on the basis of financial need.
B. Similar to a loan, a Pell grant must be repaid.
C. It is available to undergraduate students.
D. All of the above are correct.

24. Which of the following is a type of benefit plan offered by employers in which employees are permitted to choose from a list of benefits, such as life insurance and childcare, in addition to their basic pay?

A. Salary continuation plan
B. Salary reduction plan
C. Cafeteria plan
D. Excess benefit plan

25. If an individual dies "testate," which of the following is correct?

A. The decedent did not have a legally valid will at the time of death.
B. The decedent had a legally valid will at the time of death.
C. The decedent did not have a legally valid trust at the time of death.
D. The decedent had a legally valid trust at the time of death.

26. Purchasing power risk is a type of:

A. unsystematic risk.
B. systematic risk.
C. credit risk.
D. default risk.

27. Which of the following is the standard used to determine if losses from a business activity are considered active or passive in nature?

A. Active involvement standard
B. Personal contribution standard
C. Direct engagement standard
D. Material participation standard

28. The activities of daily living (ADLs) which are used to measure the functional status of an individual include all but which of the following?

A. Dressing
B. Transferring
C. Driving
D. Toileting

29. Interest earned from Series EE bonds may be excluded from gross income if proceeds are used to pay for which of the following?

A. First-time home purchase
B. Qualified higher education expenses
C. Qualified medical expenses
D. Tax bill owed to the IRS

30. Which of the following is the primary consideration when creating an emergency fund?

A. Liquidity and ease of access.
B. Achieving a high investment return.
C. Generating tax-free income.
D. Diversifying between stocks and bonds.

31. When a bond is selling at a premium to par, the yield to maturity will always be _______ the bond's coupon rate. If a bond is selling at a discount to par, the yield to maturity will always be _______ the bond's coupon rate.

A. greater than; less than
B. less than; greater than
C. greater than; equal to
D. less than; equal to

32. Which of the following is/are correct regarding powers of attorney and powers of appointment?

(1) A power of attorney is a legal document created by an individual authorizing someone else to act on his or her behalf.
(2) A power of appointment is a power given to a donee allowing him or her to dispose of the donor's property by selecting one or more beneficiaries to receive the property.

A. (1) only
B. (2) only
C. None of the above are correct.
D. All of the above are correct.

33. Which of the following are the five C's of credit that a lender considers when evaluating a borrower?

A. Character, conduct, collateral, conditions, cash
B. Competence, capital, capacity, considerations, collateral
C. Character, capital, capacity, collateral, conditions
D. Capital, credibility, circumstances, capacity, character

34. Which of the following is the process of converting an investment into a series of payments?

A. Capitalizing
B. Securitizing
C. Annuitizing
D. Monetizing

35. Which of the following are considered taxable income?

(1) Workers' compensation
(2) Child support
(3) Jury duty pay
(4) Premiums paid by an employer on $75,000 of group term life insurance

A. (1) and (3) only
B. (3) and (4) only
C. (1), (3), and (4) only
D. All of the above are correct.

36. Public education institutions can establish which of the following plans for employees?

A. 403(b) plan
B. 457 plan
C. Pension plan
D. All of the above are correct.

37. All but which of the following are correct regarding a PLUS loan?

A. It can be transferred from a parent to a student.
B. It is not based on financial need.
C. It is available to the parent of an undergraduate student up to the cost of attendance at the institution minus additional financial support received.
D. All of the above are correct.

38. Which of the following is/are correct regarding closed-end mutual funds?

(1) Closed-end mutual funds may issue new shares when an individual buys existing shares.
(2) Closed-end mutual funds may sell at a premium or discount to their net asset value.

A. (1) only
B. (2) only
C. None of the above are correct.
D. All of the above are correct.

39. Itemized deductions are reported on which of the following Schedules of IRS Form 1040?

A. Schedule A
B. Schedule B
C. Schedule C
D. Schedule D

40. If gift splitting is elected, a gift of $20,000 would be considered a gift of ______ by each spouse.

A. $10,000
B. $15,000
C. $20,000
D. $40,000

41. If a health insurance policy contains a ______ provision, the insured will no longer need to pay any percentage of medical expenses once his or her out-of-pocket expenses have reached the maximum amount specified in the policy.

A. reinsurance
B. capitation
C. stop-loss
D. retention

42. Which of the following is an employer-sponsored retirement plan, such as a 401(k) plan, that satisfies the requirements in the Internal Revenue Code for receiving tax-deferred treatment?

A. Qualified retirement plan
B. Nonqualified retirement plan
C. Defined benefit profit sharing plan
D. Defined contribution cash balance plan

43. Which of the following is a person who is legally and ethically bound to make decisions in the best interest of the client?

A. Actuary
B. Auditor
C. Fiduciary
D. Underwriter

44. If a lender offers a higher interest rate to a borrower who recently declared bankruptcy and a lower interest rate to a borrower with a high credit score, the lender is engaging in which of the following practices?

A. Behavioral scoring
B. Credit scoring
C. Risk-based pricing
D. None of the above are correct.

Rick and Gina
Statement of Financial Position
December 31, 20XX

ASSETS		LIABILITIES AND NET WORTH	
Cash/Cash Equivalents		**Liabilities**	
Checking account (R)[1]	$ 4,000	1st mortgage on home[3]	$ 83,000
Savings account (R)	55,000	Home equity loan	19,000
Money market fund (G)	21,000	Credit card balance[4]	33,000
		Car loans	28,000
Invested Assets			
Value mutual fund (JT)	$ 300,000	TOTAL LIABILITIES	$ 163,000
Common stocks (R)	395,000		
Retirement Assets			
401(k) (R)	$ 275,000		
Profit sharing plan (G)	35,000		
		NET WORTH	$1,320,000
Use Assets			
House (JT)	$ 280,000		
Personal property (JT)[2]	56,000		
Cars (JT)	62,000		
TOTAL ASSETS	$1,483,000		

1. R = Rick as owner, G = Gina as owner, JT = Joint tenants with rights of survivorship
2. Includes jewelry valued at $25,000
3. 30-year fixed-rate mortgage; principal amount last year was $86,200
4. 11.99% APR

45. If Rick dies this year, what will be the value of his gross estate for federal estate tax purposes?

A. $1,078,000
B. $1,113,000
C. $1,134,000
D. $1,256,000

46. Which of the following is a separately calculated tax that eliminates certain deductions and credits, thereby increasing an individual's tax liability?

A. Maximum allowable tax
B. Minimum allowable tax
C. Alternative maximum tax
D. Alternative minimum tax

47. Based on modern portfolio theory, which of the following securities would a rational investor select?

A. Rate of return 4%, beta 1.3
B. Rate of return 7%, beta 1.1
C. Rate of return 6%, beta 1.2
D. Rate of return 7%, beta 1.2

48. According to the reinstatement clause, an owner of a life insurance policy can reinstate his or her policy if all but which of the following occur?

A. An insurable interest still exists.
B. The insured is still insurable.
C. The policy lapsed due to non-payment of premium.
D. The policy was surrendered for its cash value.

49. A fixed-rate mortgage refers to which of the following?

A. The mortgage interest rate remains constant throughout the life of the loan.
B. The mortgage payment remains constant throughout the life of the loan, but the interest rate may change.
C. The mortgage payment and interest rate may change throughout the life of the loan, but the rate of depreciation remains constant.
D. None of the above are correct.

50. Which of the following is the risk of a retiree outliving his or her savings, pension, retirement plan, or other income source when retired?

A. Principal risk
B. Mortality risk
C. Longevity risk
D. Distribution risk

51. Which of the following is the simplest form of business ownership?

A. Partnership
B. Sole proprietorship
C. Cooperative
D. LLC

52. Which of the following is available to help eligible low-income individuals pay for the cost of health care coverage through the Health Insurance Marketplace?

A. ACA relief credit
B. Premium tax credit
C. Marketplace rebate
D. COBRA

53. Assets which pass to beneficiaries through a will are part of the decedent's:

A. probate estate.
B. ancillary estate.
C. settlement estate.
D. executor estate.

54. Which of the following may be referred to as a hybrid security because it combines features of both debt and equity?

A. Corporate bond
B. Common stock
C. Preferred stock
D. REIT

55. A waiver of premium clause:

A. waives the premium if additional insurance is purchased.
B. waives the premium in the event of disability.
C. waives the premium after a specific number of years.
D. waives the premium due to extreme financial hardship.

56. All but which of the following retirement plans are subject to required minimum distribution rules during a participant's lifetime?

A. SEP
B. Roth IRA
C. 401(k)
D. SIMPLE

57. Which of the following is the body of law that codifies all federal tax laws, including income, estate, gift, excise, alcohol, tobacco, and employment taxes?

A. Federal Revenue Act
B. Tax Reform Act
C. Internal Revenue Code
D. National Tax Code

58. All but which of the following are types of beneficiaries?

A. Charitable
B. Contingent
C. Revocable
D. All of the above are correct.

59. All but which of the following are methods of measuring yield?

A. Yield to maturity
B. Yield to call
C. Default yield
D. Current yield

60. Which of the following is the concept that as the number of policyholders increases, an insurance company's estimated losses will be closer to its actual losses?

A. Central limit theory
B. Law of large numbers
C. Law of expectations
D. Empirical rule

61. The ______ provision allows a deceased spouse's unused estate tax exclusion amount to transfer to the surviving spouse.

A. estoppel
B. portability
C. abatement
D. mobility

62. Which of the following retirement plans allows employers to make contributions toward their employees' retirement or toward their own retirement if self-employed?

A. SIMPLE IRA
B. Traditional IRA
C. Roth IRA
D. Non-deductible IRA

63. Which of the following is a reason to rent a home rather than buy?

A. The ability to deduct mortgage interest.
B. The ability to deduct property taxes.
C. The ability to build home equity.
D. None of the above are correct.

64. Dave wants to purchase a boat in 3 years. He expects to spend $15,000. If he earns an annual compound rate of return of 8% on his investments, how much should he invest at the end of each year to achieve his goal?

A. $4,278.24
B. $4,620.50
C. $4,930.91
D. $5,110.45

65. Which of the following is a retirement plan feature in which employees gain ownership over an employer contribution after a certain number of years?

A. Grading
B. Investing
C. Vesting
D. Endowing

66. Which of the following steps of the financial planning process comes directly after presenting the financial planning recommendations?

A. Understanding the client's personal and financial circumstances.
B. Analyzing the client's current course of action and potential alternate courses of action.
C. Implementing the financial planning recommendations.
D. Monitoring progress and updating.

67. All but which of the following are types of unsystematic risk?

A. Management risk
B. Regulatory risk
C. Market risk
D. Tax risk

68. Travis lives in Ohio but owns real estate in Colorado. He'd like to avoid the cost and delays of ancillary probate. Which of the following are suitable methods for Travis to achieve his goal?

(1) Revocable living trust
(2) Irrevocable trust
(3) JTWROS
(4) Testamentary trust

A. (2) only
B. (1) and (3) only
C. (1), (2), and (3) only
D. (2), (3), and (4) only

69. Which of the following is not an incident of ownership in a life insurance policy?

A. The ability to make premium payments on the policy.
B. The ability to change the beneficiary of the policy.
C. The ability to surrender or cancel the policy.
D. The ability to pledge the policy for a loan.

70. Which of the following measures the total amount of risk present in an investor's portfolio?

A. Alpha
B. Beta
C. Sharpe ratio
D. Standard deviation

71. Which of the following is correct regarding COBRA continuation coverage?

A. It may be applied to health, disability, or life insurance.
B. Evidence of insurability is not required to qualify.
C. The maximum duration of coverage is 12 months.
D. It is free if a qualifying event occurs.

72. A bank loan known as a "HELOC" is a:

A. high equity line of credit.
B. home equity line of credit.
C. home equity loan of capital.
D. health emergency line of credit.

73. Which of the following strategies involves making investment decisions that are in contrast to the prevailing market sentiment?

A. Contrarian investment strategy
B. Sector rotation strategy
C. Core and satellite investing strategy
D. Tactical asset allocation strategy

74. All but which of the following are life insurance dividend options?

A. Accumulate with interest
B. Paid-up additions
C. Premium reduction
D. Specified income

75. All but which of the following may refer to a spousal election against a will?

A. Elective share
B. Excluded share
C. Forced share
D. Statutory share

ANSWER KEY

1. B
Credit risk is the risk that a bond issuer will default.

2. A
With the tenancy in common form of property ownership, two or more individuals share ownership of a property, and the ownership shares may be unequal.

3. D
The decrease in the amount of certain tax credits above a specific income level is a phaseout.

4. D
If the gift tax annual exclusion is $18,000, an individual can gift up to that amount of present interest gifts to an unlimited number of recipients without incurring a federal gift tax.

5. C
A profit sharing plan is a type of defined contribution plan other than a pension plan. Contributions must be substantial and recurring, but are not required annually.

6. C
Chapter 13 bankruptcy is referred to as "individual debt adjustment" or the "wage earner's plan." The debtor proposes a repayment plan to make installment payments to creditors over a period of time. The debtor may use Chapter 13 bankruptcy proceedings to avoid home foreclosure. An automatic stay will stop foreclosure proceedings when a debtor files a Chapter 13 petition.

7. C
A summary prospectus is designed to provide mutual fund investors with key fund information in a clear and concise format.

8. A
Contributory negligence is the concept that if an injured party was partially responsible for causing an accident, he or she will be denied compensation for damages.

9. B
The tax filing deadline for the majority of taxpayers in the U.S. is April 15th.

10. D
An underwriter analyzes and assesses the risks associated with providing insurance to individuals and establishes the pricing of insurance premiums.

11. A
Social Security replaces a percentage of a worker's pre-retirement income based on his or her lifetime earnings.

12. B
Negative amortization will result if the periodic payments made on a loan are not enough to pay the amount of interest that accrues on the loan's principal.

13. C
Technical analysis and fundamental analysis are two common forms of analysis used by investors to evaluate markets and securities.

14. A
Gifts made during a donor's lifetime receive a carryover of basis, and gifts made at death receive a step-up in basis.

15. B
Exaggerating a loss to an insurance company to collect a larger benefit payment is considered a moral hazard.

16. D
Loans from a traditional IRA are not permitted.

17. A
When an investor buys a corporate bond, the investor lends money to the company issuing the bond. In return, the company issuing the bond commits to paying interest to the investor and also returning the principal when the bond matures.

18. D
Loan-to-value = $613,564 / $902,300 = 0.68 = 68%

19. C
REITs provide exposure to real estate. Growth stocks typically reinvest their earnings back into the company rather than pay high dividends to shareholders. GNMA securities, not FNMA, are backed by the U.S. government. Global funds invest in both U.S. and international companies.

20. A
The generation-skipping transfer tax (GSTT) is a tax on the transfer of assets to a person two or more generations younger than the donor.

21. B
Child support payments are non-deductible to the payor and tax-free to the recipient.

22. C
The store owner is reducing the chance that vandalism or theft will occur by installing shatterproof windows and a security system.

23. B
A Pell grant is an education grant distributed on the basis of financial need. Unlike a loan, a Pell grant never has to be repaid. It is available to undergraduate students.

24. C
A cafeteria plan is a type of benefit plan offered by employers in which employees are permitted to choose from a list of benefits, such as life insurance and childcare, in addition to their basic pay.

25. B
If an individual dies "testate," he or she had a legally valid will at the time of death.

26. B
Purchasing power risk is a type of systematic risk.

27. D
The material participation standard is used to determine if losses from a business activity are considered active or passive in nature.

28. C
Activities of daily living (ADLs) include dressing, transferring, toileting, eating, bathing, and maintaining continence. Driving is not considered an activity of daily living.

29. B
Interest earned from Series EE bonds may be excluded from gross income if proceeds are used to pay for qualified higher education expenses.

30. A
The primary consideration when creating an emergency fund is liquidity and ease of access.

31. B
When a bond is selling at a premium to par, the yield to maturity will always be less than the bond's coupon rate. If a bond is selling at a discount to par, the yield to maturity will always be greater than the bond's coupon rate.

32. D
A power of attorney is a legal document created by an individual authorizing someone else to act on his or her behalf. A power of appointment is a power given to a donee allowing him or her to dispose of the donor's property by selecting one or more beneficiaries to receive the property.

33. C
The five C's of credit that a lender considers when evaluating a borrower are character, capital, capacity, collateral, and conditions.

34. C
Annuitizing is the process of converting an investment into a series of payments.

35. B
Jury duty pay is taxable to the recipient. Premiums paid on up to $50,000 of group term life insurance are not considered taxable income to an employee. However, the question states that coverage is for $75,000. Therefore, a portion will be taxable. Child support payments and workers' compensation are not taxable income.

36. D
Public education institutions can establish 403(b), 457, and pension plans for employees.

37. A
A PLUS loan (parent loan for undergraduate students) is available to the parent of an undergraduate student up to the cost of attendance at the institution minus additional financial support received. It cannot be transferred from a parent to a student, and it is not based on financial need.

38. B
Closed-end mutual funds may sell at a premium or discount to their net asset value. Only open-end mutual funds may issue new shares when an individual buys existing shares.

39. A
Itemized deductions are reported on Schedule A of IRS Form 1040.

40. A
If gift splitting is elected, a gift of $20,000 would be considered a gift of $10,000 by each spouse.

41. C
If a health insurance policy contains a stop-loss provision, the insured will no longer need to pay any percentage of medical expenses once his or her out-of-pocket expenses have reached the maximum amount specified in the policy.

42. A
A qualified retirement plan is an employer-sponsored retirement plan, such as a 401(k) plan, that satisfies the requirements in the Internal Revenue Code for receiving tax-deferred treatment.

43. C
A fiduciary is a person who is legally and ethically bound to make decisions in the best interest of the client.

44. C
If a lender offers a higher interest rate to a borrower who recently declared bankruptcy and a lower interest rate to a borrower with a high credit score, the lender is engaging in risk-based pricing.

45. A

$4,000	Checking account
+ $55,000	Savings account
+ $150,000	½ Value mutual fund
+ $395,000	Common stocks
+ $275,000	401(k)
+ $140,000	½ House
+ $28,000	½ Personal property
+ $31,000	½ Cars
$1,078,000	

46. D
The alternative minimum tax (AMT) is a separately calculated tax that eliminates certain deductions and credits, thereby increasing an individual's tax liability.

47. B
B is the answer by process of elimination. Begin with the securities with a beta of 1.2 and select the one with the highest return. This eliminates security C. Next, compare the securities that have an investment return of 7% and select the one with the least risk (lowest beta). This eliminates security D. Finally, compare the two securities that remain, A and B. Security B provides a higher return for less risk than security A. Therefore, security B is the investment a rational investor would select.

48. D
If a life insurance policy is surrendered for its cash value it may not be reinstated.

49. A
With a fixed-rate mortgage, the interest rate remains constant throughout the life of the loan.

50. C
Longevity risk is the risk of a retiree outliving his or her savings, pension, retirement plan, or other income source when retired.

51. B
A sole proprietorship is the simplest form of business ownership.

52. B
A premium tax credit is available to help eligible low-income individuals pay for the cost of health care coverage through the Health Insurance Marketplace.

53. A
Assets which pass to beneficiaries through a will are part of the decedent's probate estate.

54. C
Preferred stock may be referred to as a hybrid security because it combines characteristics of both debt (fixed income investments) and equity (common stocks).

55. B
A waiver of premium clause waives the premium in the event of disability.

56. B
The lifetime required minimum distribution rules do not apply to Roth IRAs.

57. C
The Internal Revenue Code is the body of law that codifies all federal tax laws, including income, estate, gift, excise, alcohol, tobacco, and employment taxes.

58. D
Charitable, contingent, and revocable are all types of beneficiaries.

59. C
Yield to maturity, yield to call, and current yield are methods of measuring yield.

60. B
The law of large numbers is the concept that as the number of policyholders increases, an insurance company's estimated losses will be closer to its actual losses.

61. B
The portability provision allows a deceased spouse's unused estate tax exclusion amount to transfer to the surviving spouse.

62. A
A SIMPLE IRA allows employers to make contributions toward their employees' retirement or toward their own retirement if self-employed.

63. D
The choices provided would be reasons to buy a home rather than rent. Therefore, none of the choices are applicable.

64. B
FV = -$15,000
n = 3
i = 8
PV = 0
PMT = ? = $4,620.50

65. C
Vesting is a retirement plan feature in which employees gain ownership over an employer contribution after a certain number of years.

66. C
After presenting the financial planning recommendations, the next step of the financial planning process is implementing the financial planning recommendations.

67. C
Management risk, regulatory risk, and tax risk are types of unsystematic risk.

68. C
Travis can avoid probate by titling his property as joint tenants with rights of survivorship (JTWROS), placing it in a revocable living trust, or placing it in an irrevocable trust. The revocable living trust and irrevocable trust would accomplish the same objective because the revocable trust becomes irrevocable at death and avoids probate. The testamentary trust would not avoid probate because it is created by the will. Therefore, any property passing through the testamentary trust must first pass through probate.

69. A
The ability to make premium payments on a life insurance policy is not considered an incident of ownership.

70. D
Standard deviation measures the total amount of risk present in an investor's portfolio.

71. B
Evidence of insurability is not required to qualify for COBRA continuation coverage.

72. B
A bank loan known as a "HELOC" is a home equity line of credit.

73. A
A contrarian investment strategy involves making investment decisions that are in contrast to the prevailing market sentiment.

74. D
Accumulate with interest, paid-up additions, and premium reduction are life insurance dividend options. Specified income is a life insurance settlement option.

75. B
A spousal election against a will may be referred to as an elective share, forced share, or statutory share.

PRACTICE EXAM 6

QUESTIONS

1. Which of the following is a gift of personal property made through a will?

A. Testament
B. Codicil
C. Bequest
D. Endowment

2. Which of the following are backed by the full faith and credit of the government issuing the bonds and are repaid through taxes collected by the government body?

A. Revenue bonds
B. General obligation bonds
C. Convertible bonds
D. Private purpose bonds

3. Which of the following is responsible for paying estate taxes?

A. The decedent's estate
B. The beneficiary
C. The probate court
D. None of the above are correct.

4. All but which of the following are characteristics of a C corporation?

A. It is subject to double taxation.
B. It has a perpetual life.
C. It must have stock available for purchase on an exchange.
D. It is treated as a separate taxpaying entity for federal tax purposes.

5. Which of the following refers to causing an unintentional loss by failing to use reasonable care?

A. Negligence
B. Strict liability
C. Vicarious liability
D. Tort

6. If an investor earns a return of $5,000 by investing in Security A, but could have earned a return of $6,000 by investing in Security B, the $1,000 difference is the:

A. alternate forfeiture.
B. sacrifice premium.
C. value premium.
D. opportunity cost.

7. A qualified beneficiary has ______ following a qualifying event to elect COBRA continuation coverage.

A. 30 days
B. 60 days
C. 90 days
D. 180 days

8. If a fully insured worker elects to receive Social Security retirement benefits early, which of the following is correct?

A. The benefit will be temporarily reduced until the worker reaches full retirement age.
B. The benefit will be temporarily reduced until the worker reaches age 70.
C. The benefit will be permanently reduced until the spouse reaches full retirement age.
D. The benefit will be permanently reduced.

9. Which of the following is the process by which the tax basis of a tangible asset is recovered?

A. Capitalization
B. Depreciation
C. Depletion
D. Amortization

10. Which of the following is an eligible tax filing status in the United States?

A. Head of household
B. Self-employed
C. Part-time employee
D. Family caregiver

11. Which of the following is an amendment to an insurance policy that changes or adjusts coverage?

A. Rider
B. Appendix
C. Supplement
D. Schedule

12. ERISA stands for which of the following?

A. Economic Regulation and Investment Stability Act
B. Equity and Retirement Income Stability Act
C. Economic Regulations for Investments, Savings, and Assets
D. Employee Retirement Income Security Act

13. Which of the following is a regulatory form that contains information about an investment advisory firm and its operations, including business practices, conflicts of interest, and fees?

A. Investment policy statement
B. Form ADV
C. Prospectus
D. Form U4

14. Cindy gifts property equally to her three children, valued at $100,000 per gift. If her husband agrees to split the gifts, how much gift tax will Cindy be required to pay when she files her gift tax return? Assume this is the first year she's made a gift.

A. $0
B. $105,000
C. $150,000
D. $300,000

15. Which of the following is/are correct regarding use of the marital deduction?

(1) Probate is required to take full advantage of the marital deduction.
(2) The marital deduction is phased out for estates in excess of $10 million.

A. (1) only
B. (2) only
C. None of the above are correct.
D. All of the above are correct.

16. Self-employment tax consists of ______ and ______ taxes primarily for individuals who work for themselves.

A. Workers' compensation; corporate
B. Social Security; Medicare
C. Social Security; Medicaid
D. Medicare; Medicaid

17. Which of the following is an underwriting classification for individuals who pose a higher level of risk to insurance companies due to having poor health or a hazardous occupation?

A. Substandard risk
B. Standard risk
C. Preferred risk
D. None of the above are correct.

18. Kathleen, age 45, and Anthony, age 47, are a married couple who would like to make IRA contributions this year. Assume that Kathleen's earned income will be $200,000, Anthony expects to have no earned income, and the IRA contribution limit is $7,000. What are the maximum IRA contributions they're eligible to make?

A. $0 for Kathleen and $0 for Anthony.
B. $7,000 for Kathleen and $0 for Anthony.
C. $7,000 for Kathleen and $3,500 for Anthony.
D. $7,000 for Kathleen and $7,000 for Anthony.

19. Mental accounting and illusion of control are examples of:

A. cognitive errors.
B. emotional biases.
C. interpersonal communication.
D. nondirective counseling skills.

20. _______ risk cannot be eliminated through diversification because it affects the entire market. _______ risk may be diversified away or avoided by not investing in stocks that exhibit the risk.

A. Non-systematic; Unsystematic
B. Unsystematic; Systematic
C. Systematic; Unsystematic
D. Total; Systematic

21. Which of the following is calculated as a percentage of the amount invested in a mutual fund and can act as a sales commission?

A. Turnover ratio
B. Expense ratio
C. Load
D. Capital gain

22. Which of the following describes an itemized deduction?

A. A trade or business expense deductible from AGI.
B. A personal expense deductible from AGI.
C. A trade or business expense deductible in arriving at gross income.
D. A personal expense deductible in arriving at gross income.

23. After Linda (the insured) died, the insurance company discovered that she was age 58, but according to her application she claimed she was 56. Which of the following actions can the insurer take?

A. The insurer can deny paying the death benefit to Linda.
B. The insurer can cancel the policy if Linda died during the contestable period.
C. The insurer can decrease the face amount of the policy.
D. The insurer can force Linda to pay a higher premium.

24. All but which of the following are correct regarding bond mutual funds?

A. The securities that bond funds hold can vary in terms of risk, return, duration, and volatility.
B. Bond funds invest primarily in bonds or other types of debt securities.
C. Bond funds have fixed maturities which guarantees safety of principal.
D. All of the above are correct.

25. Which of the following is an account established through an employer that reimburses employees for qualified medical expenses incurred during the coverage period?

A. GIC
B. LTD
C. FML
D. FSA

26. Which of the following is the first step of the financial planning process?

A. Identifying and selecting goals.
B. Understanding the client's personal and financial circumstances.
C. Analyzing the client's current course of action and potential alternate courses of action.
D. Developing the financial planning recommendations.

27. Which of the following is a diversified mutual fund that automatically shifts toward a more conservative mix of investments as it approaches a particular year?

A. Target date fund
B. Futures fund
C. Select fund
D. Indexed target fund

28. Sole ownership of property is also known as which of the following?

A. Easement
B. Conveyance
C. Fee simple
D. None of the above are correct.

29. Which of the following represents the maximum amount of capital loss that a single taxpayer can deduct in a single year?

A. Up to the amount of capital gain.
B. Up to the amount of capital gain plus $3,000.
C. Up to the amount of capital gain plus $6,000.
D. There is no limit.

30. Which of the following is a common exclusion from a homeowners insurance policy?

A. Windstorm
B. Vandalism
C. Hail
D. Earthquake

31. All but which of the following are correct regarding real estate held as an investment?

A. It has the potential for a 1035 exchange.
B. It's considered a long-term hedge against inflation.
C. It lacks liquidity.
D. It offers tax-shelter potential.

32. Which of the following is the primary purpose of adding a call provision to a bond agreement?

A. To protect investors from a decline in interest rates.
B. To protect investors from an increase in interest rates.
C. To protect the bond issuer from a decline in interest rates.
D. To protect the bond issuer from an increase in interest rates.

33. Total debt payments should not exceed _______ of gross income.

A. 20%
B. 25%
C. 28%
D. 36%

34. Which of the following is an inflation-protected savings bond that is guaranteed to never lose value, even during deflationary periods?

A. Series A bond
B. Series E bond
C. Series H bond
D. Series I bond

35. Which of the following protects a decedent's creditors by providing them with an opportunity to have their claims heard and protects a decedent against the untimely filing of claims by his or her lifetime creditors?

A. Probate
B. Testamentary trust
C. Last will and testament
D. Qualified disclaimer

36. Which of the following are contributions that employees choose to have transferred from their paychecks into their employer-sponsored retirement accounts?

A. Matching contributions
B. Nonqualified deferrals
C. Elective deferrals
D. Taxable deposits

37. How can a life insurance policy deemed to be a modified endowment contract (MEC) be converted to a non-MEC?

A. It must satisfy the guideline and premium corridor test.
B. It must satisfy the seven-pay test.
C. It must petition the IRS for a private letter ruling.
D. Once a life insurance policy becomes a MEC, there is no way to reverse the tax treatment.

38. The amounts an individual withdraws from a traditional IRA or other retirement plan before reaching age _______ are generally considered premature distributions.

A. 59 ½
B. 63
C. 65
D. 70 ½

39. A Coverdell ESA is an:

A. employer sponsored account.
B. equity share agreement.
C. education savings account.
D. employee savings account.

40. Which of the following strategies is an investor using if she has $10,000 to invest and chooses to invest $2,000 on the first day of the month for the next five months?

A. Dollar cost averaging
B. Constant proportion portfolio investing
C. Fixed time rebalancing
D. Value averaging

41. Which of the following trusts provides a surviving spouse with a lifetime interest in trust assets and may include a right to invade principal on his or her behalf under certain conditions?

A. Marital trust
B. Credit shelter trust
C. Crummey trust
D. Estate trust

42. With a/an ______ loan, an individual borrows a sum of money and must pay it back in fixed amounts.

A. installment
B. serial
C. secured
D. revolving

43. All but which of the following are correct regarding 529 plans?

A. Contributions may be eligible for a state income tax deduction.
B. Contributions and investment earnings grow tax-free.
C. Distributions used to pay for qualified education expenses are taxed at capital gains rates.
D. All of the above are correct.

44. Reinvestment risk is a type of:

A. unsystematic risk.
B. systematic risk.
C. interest rate risk.
D. purchasing power risk.

45. Terry, while starting a bonfire on his property, negligently caused his neighbor's house to catch fire. The neighbor's insurer paid for the damage, and then sued Terry for reimbursement. Which of the following principles gives the insurer this right?

A. Absolute liability
B. Attractive nuisance
C. Subrogation
D. Estoppel

46. A fiduciary for a qualified retirement plan includes all but which of the following?

A. Plan administrator
B. Plan sponsor
C. Plan trustee
D. All of the above are correct.

47. Relating to the time value of money, the ______ is what a series of payments received in the future is worth today at a predetermined rate of interest known as the discount rate.

A. future value
B. present value
C. serial value
D. lump sum

48. Investing in index funds is most closely associated with which of the following?

A. Passive investing
B. Active investing
C. Qualitative investing
D. Quantitative investing

49. Which of the following is/are correct regarding living trusts and testamentary trusts?

(1) Living trusts come into existence only upon death.
(2) Testamentary trusts come into existence when the will is signed.

A. (1) only
B. (2) only
C. None of the above are correct.
D. All of the above are correct.

50. Which of the following is an agreement between a borrower and a lender that allows the borrower to receive a loan to purchase a home, and gives the lender the right to foreclose on the property if the borrower fails to repay the loan?

A. Conveyance
B. Pledge agreement
C. Mortgage
D. Hypothecation

51. Which of the following actions do insurers take to offset adverse selection?

A. Insurers limit coverage to increase large claims.
B. Insurers lower underwriting standards.
C. Insurers lower premiums.
D. Insurers raise premiums.

For questions 52 – 55, determine if the fringe benefit listed is taxable or non-taxable. Use only one answer per blank. Answers may be used more than once or not at all.

A. Taxable fringe benefit
B. Non-taxable fringe benefit

52. ____ Use of employer-provided on-premises athletic facilities

53. ____ Personal use of a company car, airplane, or lodging

54. ____ Working condition fringe benefits

55. ____ Employee achievement awards

56. In the regulation of financial planners and advisory firms, the acronym "RIA" designates which of the following?

A. Regulatory Investment Associate
B. Risk and Investment Analyst
C. Regulated Investment Advisor
D. Registered Investment Advisor

57. Which of the following is a collection of investments such as stocks, bonds, commodities, or real estate?

A. ADR
B. SAR
C. ETF
D. MBS

58. Property distribution during divorce is governed by which of the following systems in the United States?

A. Tenancy property and fee simple property
B. Community property and common law property
C. Community property and fee simple property
D. Civil law property and common law property

59. Which of the following is the period of time following the due date of an insurance premium payment in which the insured can still pay the premium without the policy lapsing?

A. Lapse period
B. Extension period
C. Deferred period
D. Grace period

60. All but which of the following are correct regarding open-end credit?

A. It is a type of installment credit in which money can be borrowed and paid back up to an agreed limit.
B. Interest is charged only on the borrowed amount that remains to be paid back.
C. The borrowed amount may be paid off at any time within the agreed upon period.
D. All of the above are correct.

61. Which of the following is a provision in a bond agreement that allows the issuer to retire a portion of the debt each year or at predetermined intervals?

A. Fund retirement provision
B. Sinking fund provision
C. Repayment provision
D. Debt service provision

62. Which of the following occurs when a decedent owned real property located in a state outside his or her state of residence?

A. Ancillary probate
B. Associative probate
C. Intestate probate
D. Testate probate

63. A variable life insurance policy will pay a benefit that varies according to which of the following?

A. The flexibility of premiums paid.
B. The variability of the mortality factor.
C. The value of underlying investments.
D. All of the above are correct.

64. Which of the following may be used to transition ownership of a corporation to employees by transferring shares of company stock?

A. SIMPLE
B. ESOP
C. VEBA
D. SEP

65. Nathan opened a college savings account when his son was born and deposited $4,000 into the account. Today the account has a value of $7,000. How old is Nathan's son if the deposit has been growing at an annual rate of 7% compounded annually?

A. 6 years old
B. 7 years old
C. 8 years old
D. 9 years old

66. Event risk is a type of:

A. non-diversifiable risk.
B. default risk.
C. unsystematic risk.
D. systematic risk.

67. All but which of the following are possible methods to increase estate liquidity?

A. Purchasing life insurance.
B. Designating retirement benefits to the estate.
C. Executing a buy-sell agreement.
D. All of the above are correct.

68. Treasury bills, money market funds, and short-term CDs would be classified as which of the following on the statement of financial position?

A. Fixed income funds
B. Cash equivalents
C. Bond funds
D. Alternative investments

69. All but which of the following are correct regarding zero-coupon bonds?

A. Taxable zero-coupon bonds are best positioned in taxable accounts.
B. Zero-coupon bonds have no reinvestment risk.
C. Taxes must be paid on accrued interest each year even though no interest is received by the bondholder.
D. None of the above are correct.

70. Which of the following is correct regarding a "skip person" for GSTT purposes?

A. A skip person is a related individual one or more generations younger than the transferor.
B. A skip person is a related individual two or more generations younger than the transferor.
C. A related individual cannot be a skip person.
D. None of the above are correct.

71. Candace, age 67, pays $200,000 for a fixed annuity that will pay her $20,000 per year for the rest of her life. If her life expectancy is 16 years, how much of each annual payment will be taxable?

A. $7,500
B. $12,500
C. $15,000
D. $20,000

72. Which of the following is/are correct regarding tax credits and deductions?

(1) A deduction is more beneficial to a higher-bracket taxpayer.
(2) A credit is more beneficial to a lower-bracket taxpayer.

A. (1) only
B. (2) only
C. None of the above are correct.
D. All of the above are correct.

73. All but which of the following are characteristics of a REIT?

A. A REIT is a publicly traded open-end investment company.
B. A mortgage REIT is a specific type of REIT.
C. A REIT can sell at a premium or discount to its NAV.
D. All of the above are correct.

74. Which of the following is an account that allows a minor to own securities without having to follow the formalities of a trust?

A. SPAC
B. UTMA
C. UIT
D. CMA

75. The part of Medicare that pays for hospital insurance is:

A. Part A.
B. Part B.
C. Part C.
D. Part D.

ANSWER KEY

1. C
A bequest is a gift of personal property made through a will.

2. B
General obligation bonds are backed by the full faith and credit of the government issuing the bonds and are repaid through taxes collected by the government body.

3. A
The decedent's estate is responsible for paying estate taxes.

4. C
A C corporation is subject to double taxation, has a perpetual life, and is treated as a separate taxpaying entity for federal tax purposes.

5. A
Negligence refers to causing an unintentional loss by failing to use reasonable care.

6. D
If an investor earns a return of $5,000 by investing in Security A, but could have earned a return of $6,000 by investing in Security B, the $1,000 difference is the opportunity cost.

7. B
A qualified beneficiary has 60 days following a qualifying event to elect COBRA continuation coverage.

8. D
A fully insured worker may elect to receive Social Security retirement benefits early, but with a permanently reduced monthly benefit.

9. B
Depreciation is the process by which the tax basis of a tangible asset is recovered.

10. A
The only eligible tax filing status listed is head of household.

11. A
A rider is an amendment to an insurance policy that changes or adjusts coverage.

12. D
ERISA stands for Employee Retirement Income Security Act.

13. B
Form ADV is a regulatory form that contains information about an investment advisory firm and its operations, including business practices, conflicts of interest, and fees.

14. A
Because this is the first year Cindy has made a gift, she has not gifted more than her lifetime exemption amount. Therefore, she will not owe any gift taxes.

15. C
Probate is not required to use the marital deduction. There is no marital deduction phaseout.

16. B
Self-employment tax consists of Social Security and Medicare taxes primarily for individuals who work for themselves.

17. A
Substandard risk is an underwriting classification for individuals who pose a higher level of risk to insurance companies due to having poor health or a hazardous occupation.

18. D
Kathleen can contribute $7,000 to her IRA and a spousal IRA contribution of $7,000 can be made for Anthony.

19. A
Mental accounting and illusion of control are examples of cognitive errors.

20. C
Systematic risk cannot be eliminated through diversification because it affects the entire market. Unsystematic risk may be diversified away or avoided by not investing in stocks that exhibit the risk.

21. C
A load is calculated as a percentage of the amount invested in a mutual fund and can act as a sales commission.

22. B
An itemized deduction is a personal expense deductible from AGI. It is a "below-the-line" deduction.

23. C
The insurance company can decrease the face amount of Linda's policy if she misstated her age on her application. The death benefit will be adjusted to what the premiums paid would have purchased if she had not misstated her age.

24. C
Bond funds invest primarily in bonds or other types of debt securities which can vary in terms of risk, return, duration, and volatility.

25. D
An FSA (flexible spending account) is an account established through an employer that reimburses employees for qualified medical expenses incurred during the coverage period.

26. B
The first step of the financial planning process is understanding the client's personal and financial circumstances.

27. A
A target date fund is a diversified mutual fund that automatically shifts toward a more conservative mix of investments as it approaches a particular year.

28. C
Sole ownership of property is also known as fee simple.

29. B
The maximum amount of capital loss that a single taxpayer can deduct in a single year is up to the amount of capital gain plus $3,000.

30. D
Earthquake is a common exclusion from a homeowners insurance policy.

31. A
Real estate held as an investment is considered a long-term hedge against inflation. It offers tax-shelter potential but lacks liquidity. A 1035 exchange pertains to life insurance and not real estate.

32. C
The primary purpose of adding a call provision to a bond agreement is to protect the bond issuer from a decline in interest rates.

33. D
Total debt payments should not exceed 36% of gross income.

34. D
A Series I bond is an inflation-protected savings bond that is guaranteed to never lose value, even during deflationary periods.

35. A
Probate protects a decedent's creditors by providing them with an opportunity to have their claims heard and protects a decedent against the untimely filing of claims by his or her lifetime creditors.

36. C
Elective deferrals are contributions that employees choose to have transferred from their paychecks into their employer-sponsored retirement accounts.

37. D
Once a life insurance policy becomes a modified endowment contract (MEC), there is no way to reverse the tax treatment.

38. A
The amounts an individual withdraws from a traditional IRA or other retirement plan before reaching age 59 ½ are generally considered premature distributions.

39. C
A Coverdell ESA is an education savings account.

40. A
An investor is dollar cost averaging if she has $10,000 to invest and chooses to invest $2,000 on the first day of the month for the next five months.

41. B
A credit shelter trust (B trust) provides a surviving spouse with a lifetime interest in trust assets and may include a right to invade trust principal on his or her behalf under certain conditions.

42. A
With an installment loan, an individual borrows a sum of money and must pay it back in fixed amounts.

43. C
Contributions to a 529 plan may be eligible for a state income tax deduction. Contributions and investment earnings grow tax-free, and distributions used to pay for qualified education expenses are also tax-free.

44. B
Reinvestment risk is a type of systematic risk.

45. C
Subrogation refers to an insurance company's right to seek reimbursement from the person or entity legally responsible for an accident after the insurer has paid money to the insured.

46. D
Fiduciaries for a qualified retirement plan include the plan administrator, plan sponsor, and plan trustee.

47. B
Relating to the time value of money, the present value is what a series of payments received in the future is worth today at a predetermined rate of interest known as the discount rate.

48. A
Investing in index funds is most closely associated with passive investing.

49. C
Living trusts come into existence when signed. Testamentary trusts come into existence when the provisions of the will dictate and the will is probated.

50. C
A mortgage is an agreement between a borrower and a lender that allows the borrower to receive a loan to purchase a home and gives the lender the right to foreclose on the property if the borrower fails to repay the loan.

51. D
To offset adverse selection, insurers increase underwriting standards, raise premiums, and limit coverage to reduce large claims.

52. B
Use of employer-provided on-premises athletic facilities is a non-taxable fringe benefit.

53. A
Personal use of a company car, airplane, or lodging is a taxable fringe benefit.

54. B
Working condition fringe benefits are non-taxable.

55. B
Employee achievement awards are non-taxable fringe benefits.

56. D
In the regulation of financial planners and advisory firms, the acronym "RIA" stands for Registered Investment Advisor.

57. C
An ETF (exchange-traded fund) is a collection of investments such as stocks, bonds, commodities, or real estate.

58. B
Property distribution during divorce is governed by community property and common law property systems in the United States.

59. D
The grace period is the period of time following the due date of an insurance premium payment in which the insured can still pay the premium without the policy lapsing.

60. A
Open-end credit is a type of revolving credit in which money can be borrowed and paid back up to an agreed limit. Interest is charged only on the borrowed amount that remains to be paid back, and the borrowed amount may be paid off at any time within the agreed upon period.

61. B
A sinking fund provision in a bond agreement allows the issuer to retire a portion of the debt each year or at predetermined intervals.

62. A
Ancillary probate occurs when a decedent owned real property located in a state outside his or her state of residence.

63. C
A variable life insurance policy will pay a benefit that varies according to the value of the underlying investments.

64. B
An ESOP (employee stock ownership plan) may be used to transition ownership of a corporation to employees by transferring shares of company stock.

65. D
PV = –$4,000
FV = $7,000
i = 7
PMT = 0
n = ? = 9

66. C
Event risk is a type of unsystematic risk.

67. D
Purchasing life insurance, designating retirement benefits to the estate, and executing a buy-sell agreement are all possible methods to increase estate liquidity.

68. B
Treasury bills, money market funds, and short-term CDs would be classified as cash equivalents on the statement of financial position.

69. A
Taxable zero-coupon bonds are best positioned in tax-deferred accounts. This is because taxes must be paid on accrued interest each year even though no interest is received by the bondholder. Zero-coupon bonds have no reinvestment risk.

70. B
A skip person for GSTT purposes is a related individual two or more generations younger than the transferor.

71. A
Step 1: Total payments expected = $20,000 per year × 16 years = $320,000
Step 2: Exclusion ratio = $200,000 / $320,000 = 0.625
Step 3: Taxable portion = $20,000 × (1 – 0.625) = $7,500

72. D
A deduction is more beneficial to a high-bracket taxpayer, and a credit is more beneficial to a low-bracket taxpayer.

73. A
REITs are publicly traded closed-end investment companies. A REIT can sell at a premium or discount to its NAV. A mortgage REIT is a specific type of REIT.

74. B
An UTMA (Uniform Transfers to Minors Act) account allows a minor to own securities without having to follow the formalities of a trust.

75. A
The part of Medicare that pays for hospital insurance is Part A.

PRACTICE EXAM 7

QUESTIONS

1. If an investor's portfolio has a beta of 1.0, which of the following is correct?

A. The portfolio is risk free and will move in tandem with the overall market.
B. The portfolio has systematic risk only and will move in tandem with the overall market.
C. The portfolio has unsystematic risk only and will move opposite from the overall market.
D. A beta of 1.0 indicates there is no correlation between the investor's portfolio and the overall market.

2. The income tax due for a specified period, plus or minus allowable adjustments, is the:

A. net tax liability.
B. gross tax liability.
C. adjusted gross income.
D. net income.

3. Which of the following is a type of education grant?

A. Hope grant
B. American opportunity grant
C. Pell grant
D. 529 grant

4. All but which of the following are correct regarding a health maintenance organization (HMO)?

A. It is a type of health insurance plan that usually limits coverage to care from doctors who work for or contract with the HMO.
B. It generally covers out-of-network care.
C. An HMO may require the insured to live or work in its service area to be eligible for coverage.
D. HMOs often provide integrated care and focus on prevention and wellness.

5. Putting the financial plan into action is included in which step of the financial planning process?

A. Step 3: Analyzing the client's current course of action and potential alternate courses of action.
B. Step 4: Developing the financial planning recommendations.
C. Step 5: Presenting the financial planning recommendations.
D. Step 6: Implementing the financial planning recommendations.

6. All but which of the following are correct regarding matching contributions in a retirement plan?

A. They reduce the amount that an employee can contribute to the plan from his or her salary.
B. They grow tax-free while in the plan.
C. They are taxable only when withdrawn from the plan.
D. All of the above are correct.

7. Which of the following type of stock will generally not pay large dividends because earnings are reinvested back into the company?

A. Common stock
B. Value stock
C. Growth stock
D. Blue chip stock

8. Which of the following is the public legal process by which a state or local court validates a decedent's will?

A. Abatement
B. Probate
C. Intestate
D. Testate

9. Which of the following are permitted members of an LLC?

A. Corporations
B. Other LLCs
C. Foreign entities
D. All of the above are correct.

10. With which of the following vesting schedules will an employee have no vested interest in any employer contributions until the employee completes a required number of years of service?

A. Cliff vesting
B. Graded vesting
C. Qualified vesting
D. Nonqualified vesting

11. Relating to the time value of money, which of the following is used to value a future dollar amount in present dollars?

A. Compounding
B. Discounting
C. Adjusting
D. Capitalizing

12. According to the principle of_____, an insured will only be reimbursed for the amount of his or her actual loss and cannot make a profit from the loss.

A. adhesion
B. subrogation
C. rescission
D. indemnity

13. Which of the following is correct regarding trusts?

A. The same individual can be the grantor, trustee, and beneficiary of a trust.
B. The same individual can be the grantor and trustee, but cannot also be the beneficiary of a trust.
C. The same individual can be the trustee and beneficiary, but cannot also be the grantor of a trust.
D. None of the above are correct.

14. According to the Rule of 72, how many years will it take for an investment to double if the rate of return is 8% per year?

A. 8 years
B. 9 years
C. 10 years
D. 12 years

15. Which of the following are adjustments that must be included when calculating an individual's alternative minimum tax (AMT)?

A. Tax shelters
B. Tax subsidies
C. Tax preference items
D. Tax incentive items

16. Which of the following provides information about an insured's home or automobile coverage such as policy number, liability limits, premiums, deductibles, and expiration date?

A. Prospectus
B. Declarations page
C. Endorsement page
D. None of the above are correct.

17. Affinity bias, status quo bias, and self-control bias are examples of:

A. cognitive errors.
B. money illusions.
C. mental accounting.
D. emotional biases.

18. Which of the following is the government agency that guarantees minimum pension benefits to defined benefit plan participants whose plans have terminated due to insufficient funds?

A. PBGC
B. FDIC
C. SIPC
D. CFTC

19. The share price of an open-end mutual fund is based on which of the following?

A. EPS
B. DCF
C. ROA
D. NAV

20. Rachel owned ABC stock with a basis of $10 per share. At the time of her death, the stock was worth $25 per share. What is the basis of the stock in the hands of Rachel's beneficiary?

A. $10
B. $15
C. $25
D. $35

21. The _______ is the remaining estate of a person who has died, calculated by taking the value of all assets and subtracting all debts, including funeral costs, expenses of administering the estate, and any other allowable deductions.

A. gross estate
B. probate estate
C. total estate
D. net estate

22. A core-satellite investing approach primarily involves which of the following?

A. Dividend and non-dividend paying investments
B. Long and short investments
C. Passive and active investments
D. Domestic and international investments

23. All but which of the following are life insurance settlement options?

A. Extended term
B. Period certain and life
C. Pure life or single life
D. Specified income

24. Early withdrawals from a SIMPLE IRA are subject to a _______ penalty if the withdrawals are made during the first two years of plan participation.

A. 10%
B. 15%
C. 20%
D. 25%

25. A PLUS loan is a:

A. public loan for university students.
B. parent loan for undergraduate students.
C. patient loan for uninsured services.
D. private loan for underrepresented students.

26. Which of the following is the risk that an investment will lose value due to factors that affect the overall market?

A. Financial risk
B. Market risk
C. Business risk
D. Regulatory risk

27. Which of the following is a trust created during a grantor's lifetime that can be changed or revoked at any time before death?

A. Irrevocable living trust
B. Revocable testamentary trust
C. Irrevocable inter vivos trust
D. Revocable living trust

28. Profit or loss from a business is reported on _______ of IRS Form 1040.

A. Schedule A
B. Schedule B
C. Schedule C
D. Schedule D

29. Which of the following is an education savings bond issued by the U.S. Treasury Department?

A. Series EE bond
B. Series HH bond
C. Series I bond
D. TIPS

30. To qualify for Social Security disability benefits, a worker must meet which of the following definitions of disability?

A. Unable to perform the duties of his or her own occupation.
B. Unable to perform any substantial gainful activity.
C. Unable to perform the duties of his or her own occupation for one year, then unable to perform any substantial gainful activity thereafter.
D. Unable to perform the duties of his or her own occupation for two years, then unable to perform any substantial gainful activity thereafter.

31. Which of the following is a type of account that lets an individual set aside money on a pre-tax basis to pay for qualified medical expenses?

A. HFA
B. HSA
C. TSP
D. FHA

32. Which of the following is/are correct regarding durable powers of attorney?

(1) A durable power of attorney survives the death of the principal.
(2) A durable power of attorney survives disability of both the principal and the agent.

A. (1) only
B. (2) only
C. None of the above are correct.
D. All of the above are correct.

33. In a SWOT analysis, the "S" stands for:

A. strengths.
B. strategies.
C. successes.
D. skills.

34. Which of the following type of bond can be redeemed or paid off by the issuer prior to the bond's maturity date?

A. Floating bond
B. Convertible bond
C. Secured bond
D. Callable bond

35. Which of the following will result from selling an asset for more than its adjusted basis?

A. Capital gain
B. Capital loss
C. Adjusted gain
D. Adjusted loss

36. Lee started manufacturing a new type of protective helmet that he sells at a local bike shop. He wants to protect himself from liability in case a customer sues due to a defect in the helmet. He contacts his insurance agent to purchase a liability policy. Which method of risk management is Lee using?

A. Reduction
B. Transfer
C. Retention
D. Diversification

37. Which of the following is correct regarding a required minimum distribution from a retirement plan?

A. An individual is permitted to withdraw more than the minimum required amount.
B. Any amount withdrawn in excess of the required amount is tax-free.
C. Only the amount withdrawn in excess of the required amount is taxable.
D. None of the above are correct.

38. Which of the following personal financial statements shows an individual's net worth?

A. Statement of cash flows
B. Income statement
C. Balance sheet
D. Tax return

39. Which of the following is/are correct regarding the capital structure of closed-end mutual funds?

(1) A closed-end mutual fund has a fixed number of shares that, after original issue, trade on the secondary market.
(2) The price an investor pays when buying shares of a closed-end mutual fund is the net asset value (NAV).

A. (1) only
B. (2) only
C. None of the above are correct.
D. All of the above are correct.

40. Which of the following forms of bankruptcy is also known as the "individual debt adjustment" or the "wage earner's plan"?

A. Chapter 7 bankruptcy
B. Chapter 9 bankruptcy
C. Chapter 11 bankruptcy
D. Chapter 13 bankruptcy

41. All but which of the following are types of mortgages?

A. Conventional
B. HELOC
C. Jumbo
D. Adjustable rate

42. Which of the following refers to legal ownership of a property or asset?

A. Title
B. Conveyance
C. Warranty
D. Charter

43. Which of the following is correct regarding a passive loss for tax purposes?

A. It is a personal loss in which the taxpayer did not materially participate.
B. It is a business loss in which the taxpayer did not materially participate.
C. It is a personal loss in which the taxpayer materially participated.
D. It is a business loss in which the taxpayer materially participated.

For questions 44 – 48, determine if the fringe benefit listed is taxable or non-taxable. Use only one answer per blank. Answers may be used more than once or not at all.

A. Taxable fringe benefit
B. Non-taxable fringe benefit

44. ____ Country club dues paid by an employer on behalf of an employee

45. ____ De minimis fringe benefits

46. ____ Season tickets to a sporting event

47. ____ Business use of an employer-provided automobile

48. ____ Transportation benefits such as mass transit passes or free parking at the employer's place of business

49. All but which of the following policies may permit loans from the cash value?

A. Variable life insurance
B. Universal life insurance
C. Term life insurance
D. Whole life insurance

50. Which of the following is/are correct regarding liquidity and marketability?

(1) Liquidity is the ability to sell or redeem an investment quickly and at a known price without incurring a significant loss of principal.
(2) Marketability is the speed and ease with which a security may be bought or sold.

A. (1) only
B. (2) only
C. None of the above are correct.
D. All of the above are correct.

51. Which of the following allows an individual to transfer property to a designated beneficiary without undergoing the probate process?

A. Will substitute
B. Testamentary trust
C. Titling property as tenancy in common
D. Will codicil

52. Which of the following refers to an investor's ownership stake in a company?

A. Debt
B. Bond
C. Equity
D. Capital

53. All but which of the following are types of annuities?

A. Fixed annuity
B. Variable annuity
C. Indexed annuity
D. All of the above are correct.

54. Which of the following is a qualified retirement plan in which an employee's future benefits are fixed and guaranteed?

A. Defined contribution plan
B. Defined benefit plan
C. Profit sharing plan
D. SEP

55. Which of the following refers to the interest computed on the sum of an investment's original principal plus the accrued interest?

A. Discounted interest
B. Compound interest
C. Effective interest
D. Nominal interest

56. Kelly has been investing $2,000 at the end of each 6-month period to accumulate funds for her daughter's college tuition. If the funds are earning an annual rate of 6% compounded semiannually, how much will the account be worth when Kelly's daughter begins college in 7 years?

A. $28,384.06
B. $29,235.58
C. $34,172.65
D. $35,197.83

57. Which of the following is the total amount of gifts and estate transfers exempted from an individual's gift and estate taxes owed?

A. Applicable exclusion amount
B. Gift tax annual exclusion
C. Unified testamentary amount
D. Lifetime exclusion credit

58. All but which of the following are correct regarding bonds?

A. Interest payments are determined by the bond's credit quality and duration.
B. At maturity, the bondholder receives the face value of the bond.
C. Bonds may lose value if held to maturity.
D. All of the above are correct.

59. Josh obtained a 30-year mortgage with a balance of $60,000. If the interest rate is 5.25%, the first month's interest payment will be:

A. $258.25.
B. $260.00.
C. $262.50.
D. $264.50.

60. Which of the following is referred to as "excess liability coverage"?

A. Umbrella insurance
B. Long-term care insurance
C. Malpractice insurance
D. Title insurance

61. With the ______ form of property ownership, the remaining owners do not receive the decedent's ownership interest unless specifically bequeathed by will.

A. tenancy by entirety
B. tenancy in common
C. JTWROS between spouses
D. JTWROS between non-spouses

62. The cost of employer-provided life insurance coverage up to ______ on dependents is excludable from income as a de minimis fringe benefit. The cost of coverage over the threshold is fully taxable to the employee.

A. $1,000
B. $2,000
C. $10,000
D. $50,000

63. Interest rate risk is a type of:

A. systematic risk.
B. unsystematic risk.
C. market risk.
D. purchasing power risk.

64. Bonds are sold at a ______ when they have a higher coupon rate than what is currently available in the market.

A. premium
B. discount
C. margin
D. yield

65. Which of the following is responsible for administering a decedent's estate?

A. Beneficiary
B. Financial advisor
C. Conservator
D. Executor

66. Corey's portfolio has a mean return of 12% and a standard deviation of 6%. If the risk-free rate of return is 3%, what is the portfolio's Sharpe ratio?

A. 0.5
B. 1.5
C. 2.0
D. 6.0

67. Which of the following is health insurance coverage that satisfies the Affordable Care Act's shared responsibility provision, known as the individual mandate?

A. Critical coverage
B. Benchmark coverage
C. Minimum essential coverage
D. Standardized core coverage

68. Which of the following is correct regarding the maximum amount that a homeowner may borrow through a home equity line of credit?

A. The maximum is generally a percentage of the home's appraised value plus the amount owed on the mortgage.
B. The maximum is generally a percentage of the home's appraised value minus the amount owed on the mortgage.
C. The maximum is generally a percentage of the home's appraised value without regard to the amount owed on the mortgage.
D. The maximum is based on the borrower's credit score and not the home's appraised value or mortgage balance.

69. All but which of the following are correct regarding technical analysis?

A. It assumes that security prices move in trends and countertrends.
B. It assumes that security price action is unique and non-repetitive.
C. It can be used to trade a wide range of investments such as stocks, bonds, commodities, and currencies.
D. All of the above are correct.

70. Which of the following is the amount of additional tax paid for each additional dollar of income earned?

A. Average tax rate
B. Effective tax rate
C. Marginal tax rate
D. Regressive tax rate

71. Martin designated his son, Justin, as beneficiary of his life insurance policy. This year Martin died and Justin elected to receive the $50,000 death benefit using the fixed-period option over a 10-year period. If Justin is in the 25% tax bracket, what part of each $5,000 annual payment will be taxable to him?

A. $0
B. $1,250
C. $3,750
D. $5,000

72. Which of the following is a deposit made with a financial institution for a specific period of time?

A. MBS
B. CD
C. MSA
D. CDO

73. Which of the following are relevant debt-to-income ratios for potential mortgage borrowers?

A. ROI and ROE ratios
B. EPS and P/E ratios
C. Front-end and back-end ratios
D. Current and quick ratios

74. When a person dies leaving a will, he or she dies:

A. testate.
B. intestate.
C. inter vivos.
D. testamentary.

75. Which of the following is the difference between the cost basis of company stock and its current market value?

A. Book value
B. Accumulated depreciation
C. Capital depreciation
D. Net unrealized appreciation

ANSWER KEY

1. B
If an investor's portfolio has a beta of 1.0 then it has systematic risk only and will move in tandem with the overall market.

2. A
The income tax due for a specified period, plus or minus allowable adjustments, is the net tax liability.

3. C
A Pell grant is a type of education grant.

4. B
A health maintenance organization (HMO) is a type of health insurance plan that usually limits coverage to care from doctors who work for or contract with the HMO. It generally won't cover out-of-network care except in an emergency. An HMO may require the insured to live or work in its service area to be eligible for coverage. HMOs often provide integrated care and focus on prevention and wellness.

5. D
Putting the financial plan into action is included in Step 6: Implementing the financial planning recommendations.

6. A
Matching contributions in a retirement plan do not reduce the amount that an employee can contribute to the plan from his or her salary. They grow tax-free while in the plan and are taxable only when withdrawn.

7. C
A growth stock will generally not pay a large dividend because earnings are reinvested back into the company.

8. B
Probate is the public legal process by which a state or local court validates a decedent's will.

9. D
Permitted members of an LLC include corporations, foreign entities, and other LLCs.

10. A
With a cliff vesting schedule, an employee has no vested interest in any employer contributions until the employee completes a required number of years of service.

11. B
Relating to the time value of money, discounting is used to value a future dollar amount in present dollars.

12. D
According to the principle of indemnity, an insured will only be reimbursed for the amount of his or her actual loss and cannot make a profit from the loss.

13. A
The same individual can be the grantor, trustee, and beneficiary of a trust.

14. B
72 / 8 = 9 years
By dividing 72 by the annual interest rate, an investor can determine how many years it will take for the initial investment to double.

15. C
Tax preference items are adjustments that must be included when calculating an individual's alternative minimum tax (AMT).

16. B
The declarations page provides information about an insured's home or automobile coverage such as policy number, liability limits, premiums, deductibles, and expiration date.

17. D
Affinity bias, status quo bias, and self-control bias are examples of emotional biases.

18. A
The PBGC (Pension Benefit Guaranty Corporation) is the government agency that guarantees minimum pension benefits to defined benefit plan participants whose plans have terminated due to insufficient funds.

19. D
The share price of an open-end mutual fund is based on the NAV (net asset value).

20. C
Rachel's stock receives a full step-up in basis at her death. Lifetime gifts do not receive a step-up in basis.

21. D
The net estate is the remaining estate of a person who has died, calculated by taking the value of all assets and subtracting all debts, including funeral costs, expenses of administering the estate, and any other allowable deductions.

22. C
A core-satellite investing approach primarily involves passive (core) and active (satellite) investments.

23. A
Period certain and life, pure life or single life, and specified income are life insurance settlement options.

24. D
Early withdrawals from a SIMPLE IRA are subject to a 25% penalty if the withdrawals are made during the first two years of plan participation.

25. B
A PLUS loan is a parent loan for undergraduate students.

26. B
Market risk is the risk that an investment will lose value due to factors that affect the overall market.

27. D
A revocable living trust is a trust created during a grantor's lifetime that can be changed or revoked at any time before death.

28. C
Profit or loss from a business is reported on Schedule C of IRS Form 1040.

29. A
A Series EE bond is an education savings bond issued by the U.S. Treasury Department.

30. B
To qualify for Social Security disability benefits, a worker must be unable to perform any substantial gainful activity.

31. B
An HSA (health savings account) is a type of account that lets an individual set aside money on a pre-tax basis to pay for qualified medical expenses.

32. C
A durable power of attorney does not survive the death of a principal or the disability of an agent.

33. A
In a SWOT analysis, the "S" stands for strengths.

34. D
A callable bond can be redeemed or paid off by the issuer prior to the bond's maturity date.

35. A
Selling an asset for more than its adjusted basis will result in a capital gain.

36. B
By purchasing a liability policy, Lee is transferring risk to the insurance company.

37. A
An individual is permitted to withdraw more than the minimum required amount from a retirement plan.

38. C
An individual's net worth is shown on the balance sheet.

39. A
A closed-end mutual fund has a fixed number of shares that, after original issue, trade on the secondary market. The price an investor pays when buying shares of a closed-end mutual fund is based on supply and demand.

40. D
Chapter 13 bankruptcy is also known as the "individual debt adjustment" or the "wage earner's plan."

41. B
Conventional, jumbo, and adjustable rate are types of mortgages.

42. A
Title refers to legal ownership of a property or asset.

43. B
A passive loss for tax purposes is a business loss in which the taxpayer did not materially participate.

44. A
Country club dues paid by an employer on behalf of an employee are taxable fringe benefits.

45. B
De minimis fringe benefits are non-taxable.

46. A
Free tickets to entertainment or sporting events, other than occasional or de minimis benefits, are taxable.

47. B
Business use of an employer-provided automobile is a non-taxable fringe benefit.

48. B
Transportation benefits such as mass transit passes or free parking at the employer's place of business are non-taxable fringe benefits.

49. C
Variable, universal, and whole life insurance policies may permit loans from the cash value. Loans are not permitted from term policies because there is no cash value.

50. D
Liquidity is the ability to sell or redeem an investment quickly and at a known price without incurring a significant loss of principal. Marketability is the speed and ease with which a security may be bought or sold.

51. A
A will substitute allows an individual to transfer property to a designated beneficiary without undergoing the probate process.

52. C
Equity refers to an investor's ownership stake in a company.

53. D
Types of annuities include fixed, variable, and indexed.

54. B
A defined benefit plan is a qualified retirement plan in which an employee's future benefits are fixed and guaranteed.

55. B
Compound interest is the interest computed on the sum of an investment's original principal plus the accrued interest.

56. C
PMT = -$2,000
n = 7 × 2 = 14
i = 6 / 2 = 3
PV = 0
FV = ? = $34,172.65

57. A
The applicable exclusion amount is the total amount of gifts and estate transfers exempted from an individual's gift and estate taxes owed.

58. C
Interest payments are determined by the bond's credit quality and duration. At maturity, the bondholder receives the face value of the bond. Bonds will not lose value if held to maturity.

59. C
Step 1: Annual interest = $60,000 × 0.0525 = $3,150
Step 2: Monthly interest = $3,150 / 12 months = $262.50

60. A
Umbrella insurance is referred to as "excess liability coverage."

61. B
With the tenancy in common form of property ownership, the remaining owners do not receive the decedent's ownership interest unless specifically bequeathed by will.

62. B
The cost of employer-provided life insurance coverage up to $2,000 on dependents is excludable from income as a de minimis fringe benefit. The cost of coverage over $2,000 is fully taxable to the employee.

63. A
Interest rate risk is a type of systematic risk.

64. A
Bonds are sold at a premium when they have a higher coupon rate than what is currently available in the market.

65. D
An executor is responsible for administering a decedent's estate.

66. B
$S_h = (R_p - R_f) / S_p$
$S_h = (12\% - 3\%) / (6\%) = 1.5$

67. C
Minimum essential coverage is health insurance coverage that satisfies the Affordable Care Act's shared responsibility provision, known as the individual mandate.

68. B
The maximum amount that a homeowner may borrow through a home equity line of credit is generally a percentage of the home's appraised value minus the amount owed on the mortgage.

69. B
Technical analysis assumes that security prices move in trends and countertrends, and that price action is repetitive, with certain patterns reoccurring. It can be used to trade a wide range of investments such as stocks, bonds, commodities, and currencies.

70. C
The marginal tax rate is the amount of additional tax paid for each additional dollar of income earned.

71. A
The $5,000 annual payment is not taxable to Justin, but any amount received in excess of $5,000 will be taxable.

72. B
A CD (certificate of deposit) is a deposit made with a financial institution for a specific period of time.

73. C
Front-end and back-end ratios are relevant debt-to-income ratios for potential mortgage borrowers.

74. A
When a person dies leaving a will, he or she dies testate.

75. D
Net unrealized appreciation (NUA) is the difference between the cost basis of company stock and its current market value.

PRACTICE EXAM 8

QUESTIONS

1. Which of the following are the three categories of hazards?

A. Perils, liabilities, risks
B. Life, disability, long-term care
C. Property, casualty, physical
D. Moral, morale, physical

2. A power of appointment is ______ if the holder can benefit herself, her estate, or her lifetime creditors.

A. limited
B. specific
C. general
D. private

3. Which of the following is the U.S. Individual Income Tax Return?

A. IRS Form 706
B. IRS Form 1040
C. IRS Form 1099
D. IRS Form 1120

4. Relating to the time value of money, a/an ______ will result in a higher account balance in the future.

A. callable annuity
B. convertible annuity
C. ordinary annuity
D. annuity due

5. Which of the following steps of the financial planning process comes directly after developing the financial planning recommendations?

A. Presenting the financial planning recommendations.
B. Analyzing the client's current course of action and potential alternate courses of action.
C. Implementing the financial planning recommendations.
D. Monitoring progress and updating.

6. Which of the following is correct regarding a Statement of Additional Information (SAI)?

A. It is a document provided as a supplement to a mutual fund prospectus.
B. Funds are not required to provide investors with an SAI, but they must provide it for free upon request.
C. It provides more detailed information about fund policies, operations, and risks.
D. All of the above are correct.

7. Which of the following is the total value of a decedent's estate after deducting administrative expenses, funeral costs, creditors' claims, and casualty losses?

A. Tentative taxable estate
B. Adjusted gross estate
C. Probate estate
D. Gross estate

8. Ava, age 16, works after school in her mother's bakery. Her mother owns and operates the business as a sole proprietorship. Ava is paid $15,000 per year for her work. What is Ava's tax bracket for the majority of her earnings?

A. Ava's own tax bracket.
B. Her mother's tax bracket.
C. There is no tax bracket because of the kiddie tax rules.
D. There is no tax bracket because the income is tax-free.

9. If an individual would like to protect herself not only against becoming totally disabled, but also against a reduction in income if she's forced to work fewer hours due to partial disability, which of the following provisions should be included in her disability policy?

A. Waiver of premium
B. Cost-of-living adjustment
C. Residual disability benefits
D. Change of occupation

10. With the tenancy by entirety form of property ownership, which of the following occurs when one owner dies?

A. The decedent's share is distributed directly to the surviving spouse, and the property goes to probate.
B. The decedent's share is distributed directly to the surviving spouse, and the property avoids probate.
C. The decedent's share is distributed according to the will, and the property goes to probate.
D. The decedent's share is distributed according to the will, and the property avoids probate.

11. Which of the following is a type of cognitive error in behavioral finance that occurs when individuals treat their money differently depending on the source of the funds or how they intend to use it?

A. Affinity bias
B. Illusion of control
C. Money illusion
D. Mental accounting

12. All but which of the following are correct regarding modern portfolio theory?

A. For a given level of risk, investors prefer higher returns to lower returns.
B. Investors are irrational and naturally tolerant of a high degree of risk.
C. Increased risk is an inherent part of achieving higher returns.
D. All of the above are correct.

13. Which of the following is correct regarding the generation-skipping transfer tax (GSTT)?

A. A generation-skipping transfer may occur during the transferor's lifetime only.
B. A generation-skipping transfer may occur after the transferor's death only.
C. A generation-skipping transfer may occur during the transferor's lifetime or at death.
D. None of the above are correct.

14. All but which of the following are elements of an insurable risk?

A. The loss must be due to chance.
B. The loss must be catastrophic.
C. There must be a large number of exposure units to make losses reasonably predictable.
D. The loss must be definite and measurable.

15. Which of the following represents how much a fund pays for portfolio management, administration, marketing, and distribution expenses?

A. Turnover ratio
B. Regulatory fees
C. Front-end load
D. Expense ratio

16. Which of the following is the process of selecting, classifying, and pricing applicants for insurance?

A. Underwriting
B. Indemnifying
C. Risk mitigating
D. Risk pooling

17. A bond has a market price of $920 and a face value of $1,000. If the bond pays a 12% semiannual coupon payment and matures in 4 years, what is its yield to maturity?

A. 14.72%
B. 15.19%
C. 16.37%
D. 17.68%

18. Which of the following is/are correct regarding the lifetime learning credit and the American opportunity credit?

(1) Only the lifetime learning credit is phased out for high-income taxpayers.
(2) The lifetime learning credit cannot be used in the same year as the American opportunity credit.

A. (1) only
B. (2) only
C. None of the above are correct.
D. All of the above are correct.

19. COBRA continuation coverage may provide for the extension of health insurance coverage under certain circumstances up to a maximum of _______ months.

A. 36
B. 48
C. 60
D. 72

20. All but which of the following entities will protect owners from liability beyond the amount they personally invested?

A. LLC
B. C corporation
C. S corporation
D. Sole proprietorship

21. Tony makes a lifetime gift of stock valued at $28,000 (basis of $20,000) to his cousin, Charles. Three years later, Charles makes a lifetime gift of the same stock, now worth $35,000, to his brother, Jerry. What is Jerry's basis?

A. $7,000
B. $15,000
C. $20,000
D. $35,000

22. Which of the following is the process of paying off a loan with periodic payments, so that the amount of principal owed decreases with each payment?

A. Amortization
B. Negative amortization
C. Impairment
D. Depreciation

23. Which of the following types of coverage may be provided by long-term care policies?

(1) Skilled nursing care
(2) Intermediate nursing care
(3) Home health care
(4) Custodial care

A. (1) and (4) only
B. (3) and (4) only
C. (1), (2), and (3) only
D. All of the above are correct.

24. A _______ loan is a mortgage that is not insured or guaranteed by the U.S. government.

A. conventional
B. nonconventional
C. conforming
D. nonconforming

25. Which of the following is/are correct regarding corporate bonds?

(1) Coupon rates are determined by the credit quality of the corporation.
(2) As credit quality increases, coupon rates will also increase.

A. (1) only
B. (2) only
C. None of the above are correct.
D. All of the above are correct.

26. Which of the following is the original price that an asset was acquired for?

A. Basis point
B. Depreciated basis
C. Cost basis
D. Amortized basis

27. "Strategic" and "tactical" are types of:

A. profit sharing plans.
B. pension plans.
C. technical analysis.
D. asset allocation strategies.

28. Which of the following would be considered an inter vivos transfer?

A. A transfer that occurs upon the death of the grantor.
B. A transfer that occurs during the life of the grantor.
C. Any transfer that occurs between two related parties.
D. Any transfer that occurs between two unrelated parties.

29. Unsystematic risk is also known as:

A. market risk.
B. non-diversifiable risk.
C. diversifiable risk.
D. PRIME risk.

30. All but which of the following are correct regarding dividends paid from a life insurance policy?

A. Dividends distributed from a permanent life insurance policy will be tax-free to the extent they exceed the premiums paid to date.
B. Policy dividends are partly a return of a deliberate overcharge of premium by the insurer.
C. A life insurance policy that pays a dividend is a participating policy.
D. All of the above are correct.

31. Which of the following is a guide that can offer an objective course of action to be followed during periods of stock market disruption when emotional responses might otherwise lead to poor investment decisions?

A. Form ADV
B. Investment policy statement
C. Summary prospectus
D. Risk tolerance questionnaire

32. Property that is transferred into a trust is known as the:

A. bequest.
B. corpus.
C. devise.
D. endowment.

33. Which of the following are taxed as ordinary income?

A. Short-term capital losses
B. Long-term capital losses
C. Short-term capital gains
D. Long-term capital gains

34. All but which of the following factors can affect a Marketplace health insurance plan's monthly premium?

A. Location
B. Age
C. Tobacco use
D. Gender

35. Which of the following is an employer-sponsored retirement plan, usually offered by municipalities and government entities, that allows employees to defer a portion of their compensation on a tax-advantaged basis?

A. 401(k) plan
B. 403(b) plan
C. 457 plan
D. 529 plan

36. Which of the following Acts prohibits debt collection companies from using abusive, unfair, or deceptive practices to collect debts?

A. Truth in Lending Act (TILA)
B. Fair and Accurate Credit Transactions Act (FACTA)
C. Fair Credit Billing Act (FCBA)
D. The Fair Debt Collection Practices Act (FDCPA)

The following information relates to questions 37 – 38.

Nancy has a 30-year mortgage with a current balance of $240,000 and an interest rate of 5.5%. Her house was recently appraised for $320,000.

37. What is the amount of equity in Nancy's house?

A. $80,000
B. $185,000
C. $275,000
D. $460,000

38. What is Nancy's debt-to-equity ratio?

A. 1:4
B. 1:3
C. 3:1
D. 4:1

39. Which of the following is a type of endorsement in which the insured is indemnified by his or her own insurance company for losses, regardless of the source or cause of the loss?

A. Gap insurance endorsement
B. Excess liability endorsement
C. Subrogation endorsement
D. No-fault endorsement

40. Which of the following is a fiduciary arrangement in which a right to the beneficial enjoyment of property is held by another party who actually holds legal title?

A. Will
B. Trust
C. Power of attorney
D. Power of appointment

41. Which of the following is a dollar-for-dollar amount that a taxpayer claims on his or her tax return to reduce the amount of income tax owed?

A. Grant
B. Deduction
C. Credit
D. Exclusion

42. All but which of the following are characteristics of whole life insurance?

A. Premiums remain level and are guaranteed for the life of the policy.
B. Policies are required to pay dividends.
C. The death benefit is fixed.
D. It is considered permanent insurance.

43. Which of the following is a defined contribution plan that invests primarily in company stock?

A. ESOP
B. TSP
C. CESA
D. SEP

44. All but which of the following are correct regarding the duration of a bond?

A. By matching a portfolio's bond duration to the investment time horizon, an investor will increase interest rate risk.
B. The duration of a zero-coupon bond is greater than the bond's term to maturity.
C. The duration of a coupon bond is equal to the bond's term to maturity.
D. None of the above are correct.

45. A mutual fund that seeks to track the S&P 500 is a/an:

A. sector fund.
B. global fund.
C. index fund.
D. small cap fund.

46. Which of the following may cause a will to be considered invalid?

(1) The testator was influenced by another person.
(2) The testator did not have adequate mental capacity to execute a will.

A. (1) only
B. (2) only
C. None of the above are correct.
D. All of the above are correct.

47. Adjusted gross income (AGI) is the result of which of the following?

A. Gross income minus allowable deductions.
B. Gross income plus allowable deductions.
C. Gross income minus allowable credits.
D. Gross income plus allowable credits.

48. All but which of the following are correct regarding qualified retirement plans?

A. Employer and employee contributions and investment earnings grow tax-free until distributed.
B. Employee withdrawals are generally not permitted before age 65 without incurring a 15% penalty.
C. Two types of qualified retirement plans are defined contribution plans and defined benefit plans.
D. All of the above are correct.

49. Credit risk is a type of:

A. finance risk.
B. non-diversifiable risk.
C. systematic risk.
D. unsystematic risk.

50. A traditional IRA may be established and funded any time before ______ of the calendar year following the year in which the contribution applies.

A. April 15
B. June 15
C. October 31
D. December 31

51. Credit cards and home equity lines of credit are examples of:

A. commercial credit.
B. fixed-rate credit.
C. revolving credit.
D. installment credit.

52. Which of the following forms of investment analysis is used to evaluate a stock by examining the underlying company's business as well as conditions within its industry and sector?

A. Quantitative analysis
B. Technical analysis
C. Fundamental analysis
D. Market sentiment analysis

53. All but which of the following are considered non-taxable gifts and do not require payment of gift tax?

A. Gifts to a spouse.
B. Medical expenses paid directly to a medical care provider on behalf of another individual.
C. Tuition paid directly to an educational institution on behalf of another individual.
D. Mortgage payments made directly to a lender on behalf of another individual.

54. Which of the following is a corporation owned by an individual or small group of shareholders who are often members of the same family?

A. Limited partnership
B. Closely held corporation
C. Cooperative
D. Holding company

55. When must an insurable interest exist for life insurance?

A. At the time the policy is written.
B. At the time the loss is claimed.
C. At the time the policy is written and at the time the loss is claimed.
D. An insurable interest is not required for life insurance.

56. Silvia purchased a 5-year bond that pays a 3.5% semiannual coupon payment. The bond is priced at $97 per $100 of par value. What is the bond's current yield?

A. 3.50%
B. 3.61%
C. 7.22%
D. 7.65%

57. Which of the following is a form of bankruptcy that allows a debtor with earned income to develop a plan to repay all or part of his or her debts?

A. Chapter 7
B. Chapter 11
C. Chapter 12
D. Chapter 13

58. The retirement account known as a "SIMPLE" is a:

A. Securities Investment Management Plan for Employers.
B. Strategic Investment Management Plan for Employees.
C. Savings Incentive Match Plan for Employees.
D. Savings and Investment Match Plan for Employers.

59. Higher inflation = ______ interest rates = ______ bond values

A. lower; lower
B. higher; higher
C. lower; higher
D. higher; lower

60. If a qualified disclaimer is made, the beneficiary that disclaims is considered to have ______ the property and ______ a subsequent gift.

A. received; received
B. received; made
C. never received; has not made
D. never received; has made

61. Which of the following is a type of employer-provided life insurance that provides coverage for a specified number of years?

A. Group variable life insurance
B. Group term life insurance
C. Group universal life insurance
D. Group whole life insurance

62. Which of the following measures the risk-adjusted performance of a non-diversified portfolio?

A. Standard deviation
B. Alpha
C. Sharpe ratio
D. Yield

63. A worker's ______ is the age when he or she is entitled to receive full Social Security retirement benefits.

A. FRA
B. PIA
C. SSA
D. TWA

64. Which of the following is/are correct regarding an ABLE account?

(1) An ABLE account is intended to be used to pay for qualified disability-related expenses, such as education, housing, and transportation.
(2) There is no age requirement related to the onset of disability to be eligible to establish an ABLE account.

A. (1) only
B. (2) only
C. None of the above are correct.
D. All of the above are correct.

65. Which of the following is an unsystematic form of investment risk inherent in company operations?

A. Exchange rate risk
B. Purchasing power risk
C. Market risk
D. Business risk

66. Which of the following is correct regarding gifts of a present interest?

A. They are ineligible for the generation-skipping transfer tax.
B. They are eligible for the gift tax annual exclusion.
C. They are treated the same as gifts of a future interest for the gift tax annual exclusion.
D. They include gifts of a remainer interest.

67. All but which of the following are correct regarding the entity-purchase form of a buy-sell agreement?

A. The business entity purchases life insurance on the lives of each business owner.
B. Life insurance proceeds provide the business entity with money to buy the deceased owner's business interest from his or her estate.
C. Each business owner pays the premiums for life insurance.
D. If a company has three owners, then three life insurance policies will be purchased by the business.

68. Which of the following are correct regarding vesting schedules for employee contributions to a 401(k) plan and the investment earnings on those contributions?

A. Employees are always 50% vested in their own contributions and any earnings from those contributions.
B. Employees are always 100% vested in their own contributions and any earnings from those contributions.
C. Vesting for employee contributions and any earnings from those contributions varies by plan.
D. None of the above are correct.

69. Household goods, furniture, jewelry, appliances, and artwork are examples of which of the following?

A. Tangible personal property
B. Nonpersonal realty
C. Real property
D. All of the above are correct.

70. Which of the following is/are correct regarding fully funded pension plans?

(1) A defined benefit plan is considered fully funded if it has enough assets to pay all benefits that have been earned under the plan.
(2) A plan's funded status can vary depending on the method used to value the plan's assets and liabilities.

A. (1) only
B. (2) only
C. None of the above are correct.
D. All of the above are correct.

71. Which of the following allows shareholders to vote for corporate directors and on other matters affecting the company without having to personally attend shareholder meetings?

A. Common voting
B. Preferred voting
C. Proxy voting
D. Deputy voting

72. Which of the following is a type of life insurance that offers flexible premiums, a flexible death benefit, and investment flexibility?

A. Second-to-die life insurance
B. Variable life insurance
C. Universal life insurance
D. Variable universal life insurance

73. Which of the following is a qualified retirement plan in which an employee's future benefits are variable?

A. Government pension plan
B. Defined benefit plan
C. Defined contribution plan
D. None of the above are correct.

74. All but which of the following are included in a decedent's gross estate?

A. Property subject to a general power of appointment on the date of death.
B. Property owned by a decedent's spouse on the date of death.
C. Retirement plans and annuities.
D. Transfers taking effect at death.

75. Which of the following is correct regarding reverse mortgages?

A. The loan is repaid when the borrower no longer lives in the home.
B. Interest and fees are subtracted from the loan balance each month and the balance decreases.
C. Homeowners are not required to pay property taxes or have homeowners insurance.
D. All of the above are correct.

ANSWER KEY

1. D
The three categories of hazards are moral, morale, and physical.

2. C
A power of appointment is general if the holder can benefit herself, her estate, or her lifetime creditors.

3. B
IRS Form 1040 is the U.S. Individual Income Tax Return.

4. D
Relating to the time value of money, an annuity due will result in a higher account balance in the future.

5. A
After developing the financial planning recommendations, the next step of the financial planning process is presenting the financial planning recommendations.

6. D
A Statement of Additional Information (SAI) is a document provided as a supplement to a mutual fund prospectus. It provides more detailed information about fund policies, operations, and risks. Funds are not required to provide investors with an SAI, but they must provide it for free upon request.

7. B
The adjusted gross estate is the total value of a decedent's estate after deducting administrative expenses, funeral costs, creditors' claims, and casualty losses.

8. A
Ava's income is earned, so the kiddie tax rules don't apply.

9. C
The residual disability benefits provision should be included in the disability policy because it covers partial disability.

10. B
With the tenancy by entirety form of property ownership, when one owner dies, his or her share is distributed directly to the surviving spouse, and the property avoids probate.

11. D
Mental accounting is a type of cognitive error in behavioral finance that occurs when individuals treat their money differently depending on the source of the funds or how they intend to use it.

12. B
According to modern portfolio theory, for a given level of risk, investors prefer higher returns to lower returns. Increased risk is an inherent part of achieving higher returns, and investors are rational and naturally risk averse.

13. C
A generation-skipping transfer may occur during the transferor's lifetime or at death.

14. B
The elements of an insurable risk are:
1. The loss must be due to chance.
2. The loss cannot be catastrophic.
3. There must be a large number of exposure units to make losses reasonably predictable.
4. The loss must be definite and measurable.

15. D
The expense ratio represents how much a fund pays for portfolio management, administration, marketing, and distribution expenses.

16. A
Underwriting is the process of selecting, classifying, and pricing applicants for insurance.

17. A
PV = -$920
n = 4 × 2 = 8
PMT = $1,000 × 0.12 = $120, then $120 / 2 = $60
FV = $1,000
i = ? = 7.3584 × 2 = 14.72

18. B
Both the lifetime learning credit and the American opportunity credit are phased out for high-income taxpayers. The lifetime learning credit cannot be used in the same year as the American opportunity credit.

19. A
COBRA continuation coverage may provide for the extension of health insurance coverage under certain circumstances up to a maximum of 36 months. (The maximum COBRA benefit period is 36 months if the qualifying event is death or divorce from a covered employee.)

20. D
A sole proprietorship does not provide liability protection. The C corporation, S corporation, and LLC will protect owners from liability beyond the amount personally invested.

21. C
Because these were both lifetime gifts, Tony's basis of $20,000 carries over to Charles and then to Jerry.

22. A
Amortization is the process of paying off a loan with periodic payments, so that the amount of principal owed decreases with each payment.

23. D
The basic types of coverage provided by long-term care policies are skilled nursing care, intermediate nursing care, home health care, custodial care, assisted living, adult day care, and hospice care.

24. A
A conventional loan is a mortgage that is not insured or guaranteed by the U.S. government. (Conventional loans can be conforming or nonconforming.)

25. A
Coupon rates of corporate bonds are determined by the credit quality of the corporation. As credit quality increases, coupon rates will decrease.

26. C
The original price that an asset was acquired for is its cost basis.

27. D
"Strategic" and "tactical" are types of asset allocation strategies.

28. B
An inter vivos transfer is a transfer that occurs during the life of the grantor. (Inter vivos is a Latin phrase that means "while alive.")

29. C
Unsystematic risk is also known as diversifiable risk.

30. A
Dividends distributed from a permanent life insurance policy will be taxed as ordinary income to the extent they exceed the premiums paid to date. Policy dividends are partly a return of a deliberate overcharge of premium by the insurer. A life insurance policy that pays a dividend is a participating policy.

31. B
An investment policy statement (IPS) is a guide that can offer an objective course of action to be followed during periods of stock market disruption when emotional responses might otherwise lead to poor investment decisions.

32. B
Property that is transferred into a trust is known as the corpus.

33. C
Short-term capital gains are taxed as ordinary income.

34. D
A Marketplace health insurance plan's monthly premium can be affected by location, age, tobacco use, plan category, and whether the plan covers dependents.

35. C
A 457 plan is an employer-sponsored retirement plan, usually offered by municipalities and government entities, that allows employees to defer a portion of their compensation on a tax-advantaged basis.

36. D
The Fair Debt Collection Practices Act (FDCPA) prohibits debt collection companies from using abusive, unfair, or deceptive practices to collect debts.

37. A
Owner's equity = $320,000 – $240,000 = $80,000

38. C
Step 1: Owner's equity = $320,000 – $240,000 = $80,000
Step 2: Debt-to-equity = $240,000 / $80,000 = 3:1

39. D
A no-fault endorsement is a type of endorsement in which the insured is indemnified by his or her own insurance company for losses, regardless of the source or cause of the loss.

40. B
A trust is a fiduciary arrangement in which a right to the beneficial enjoyment of property is held by another party who actually holds legal title.

41. C
A credit is a dollar-for-dollar amount that a taxpayer claims on his or her tax return to reduce the amount of income tax owed.

42. B
Whole life insurance is considered permanent insurance. The premiums remain level and are guaranteed for the life of the policy, and the death benefit is fixed. There is no requirement that whole life insurance policies must pay dividends.

43. A
An ESOP (employee stock ownership plan) is a defined contribution plan that invests primarily in company stock.

44. D
By matching a portfolio's bond duration to the investment time horizon, an investor can reduce interest rate risk. The duration of a zero-coupon bond is equal to the bond's term to maturity. The duration of a coupon bond is less than the bond's term to maturity.

45. C
A mutual fund that seeks to track the S&P 500 is an index fund.

46. B
A will may be considered invalid if the testator did not act of his or her own free will, or if the testator did not have adequate mental capacity to execute a will. Merely being influenced by another person, such as a spouse or child, will not cause a will to be considered invalid.

47. A
Adjusted gross income (AGI) is the result of gross income minus allowable deductions.

48. B
For qualified retirement plans, employer and employee contributions and investment earnings grow tax-free until distributed. Employee withdrawals are generally not permitted before age 59 ½ without incurring a 10% penalty. Two types of qualified retirement plans are defined contribution plans and defined benefit plans.

49. D
Credit risk is a type of unsystematic risk.

50. A
A traditional IRA may be established and funded any time before April 15 of the calendar year following the year in which the contribution applies.

51. C
Credit cards and home equity lines of credit are examples of revolving credit.

52. C
Fundamental analysis is generally used to evaluate a stock by examining the underlying company's business as well as conditions within its industry and sector.

53. D
Gifts that are considered non-taxable and do not require payment of gift tax include gifts to a spouse, medical expenses paid directly to a medical care provider on behalf of another individual, and tuition paid directly to an educational institution on behalf of another individual.

54. B
A corporation owned by an individual or small group of shareholders who are often members of the same family is a closely held corporation.

55. A
For life insurance, an insurable interest must only exist at the time the policy is written.

56. B
Current yield = sum of coupon payments / market price
Current yield = ($100 × 0.035) / $97 = 0.0361 = 3.61%

57. D
Chapter 13 bankruptcy allows a debtor with earned income to develop a plan to repay all or part of his or her debts.

58. C
A "SIMPLE" is a Savings Incentive Match Plan for Employees.

59. D
Higher inflation = higher interest rates = lower bond values

60. C
If a qualified disclaimer is made, the beneficiary that disclaims is considered to have never received the property and has not made a subsequent gift.

61. B
Group term life insurance is a type of employer-provided life insurance that provides coverage for a specified number of years.

62. C
The Sharpe ratio measures the risk-adjusted performance of a non-diversified portfolio.

63. A
A worker's FRA (full retirement age) is the age when he or she is entitled to receive full Social Security retirement benefits.

64. A
An ABLE account is intended to be used to pay for qualified disability-related expenses, such as education, housing, and transportation. To be eligible to establish an ABLE account, the onset of disability must occur before turning 26 years of age.

65. D
Business risk is an unsystematic form of investment risk inherent in company operations.

66. B
Gifts of a present interest are eligible for the gift tax annual exclusion. Gifts of a future interest are ineligible for the gift tax annual exclusion.

67. C
With the entity-purchase form of a buy-sell agreement, the business entity purchases life insurance on the lives of each business owner. For example, if a company has three owners, then three life insurance policies will be purchased by the business. The business pays the premiums for life insurance. The life insurance proceeds provide the business with money to buy the deceased owner's business interest from his or her estate.

68. B
Employees are always 100% vested in their own contributions to a 401(k) plan and in any earnings from those contributions.

69. A
Household goods, furniture, jewelry, appliances, and artwork are examples of tangible personal property.

70. D
A defined benefit plan is considered fully funded if it has enough assets to pay all benefits that have been earned under the plan. A plan's funded status can vary depending on the method used to value the plan's assets and liabilities.

71. C
Proxy voting allows shareholders to vote for corporate directors and on other matters affecting the company without having to personally attend shareholder meetings.

72. D
Variable universal life insurance is a type of life insurance that offers flexible premiums, a flexible death benefit, and investment flexibility.

73. C
A defined contribution plan is a qualified retirement plan in which an employee's future benefits are variable.

74. B

Property owned by the decedent's spouse on the date of death would not be included in the decedent's gross estate.

75. A

With a reverse mortgage, the loan is repaid when the borrower no longer lives in the home. Interest and fees are added to the loan balance each month and the balance grows. Homeowners are required to pay property taxes and have homeowners insurance.

PRACTICE EXAM 9

QUESTIONS

1. Which of the following allows a borrower to defer making principal payments for a set time, typically seven to ten years?

A. Graduated mortgage
B. Adjustable-rate mortgage
C. Interest-only mortgage
D. Reverse mortgage

2. Which of the following trusts may be used to reduce estate taxes between married couples?

A. A-trust, B-trust, QTIP trust
B. Marital trust, bypass trust, C-trust
C. A-trust, credit shelter trust, current income trust
D. All of the above are correct.

3. A $1,000 bond with a 4.5% coupon will pay a bondholder ______ per year.

A. $4.50
B. $9.00
C. $45.00
D. $90.00

4. All but which of the following are characteristics of a REIT?

A. Losses cannot be passed through to investors to deduct personally.
B. REIT shareholders are subject to double taxation.
C. REITs can be purchased in small denominations.
D. All of the above are correct.

5. An insurance agent represents the _____, and a broker represents the _____.

A. insurer; customer
B. customer; insurer
C. customer; customer
D. insurer; insurer

6. In a SWOT analysis, the "O" stands for:

A. obstacles.
B. objectives.
C. outcomes.
D. opportunities.

7. Which of the following is a retirement plan contribution made by an employer for each eligible employee, regardless of whether the employee decides to make a salary deferral to the account?

A. Elective contribution
B. Nonelective contribution
C. Matching contribution
D. Vesting contribution

8. Relating to the time value of money, a/an ______ is when a payment is made at the end of the period.

A. serial annuity
B. graduated annuity
C. ordinary annuity
D. annuity due

9. The efficient market hypothesis suggests all but which of the following?

A. Investors are unable to outperform the stock market on a consistent basis.
B. Any excess returns are temporary and will regress to the mean.
C. The stock market's efficiency in valuing securities is rapid and accurate.
D. Daily fluctuations in stock prices are a result of modern portfolio theory.

10. Which of the following is a gift in which the donee's right to use, possess, and enjoy the property and income derived from the property does not begin until a future date?

A. Present interest gift
B. Future interest gift
C. Inter vivos gift
D. Reversionary gift

11. All but which of the following are correct regarding alimony payments?

A. For payments to qualify as alimony, the two parties cannot file a joint tax return or live together at the time of payment.
B. Payments must be received for the benefit of the recipient.
C. Payments may be made in property rather than cash.
D. Payments cannot continue beyond the death of the recipient.

12. A professional, such as a physician, who can cause bodily harm to another may require ______ insurance. A professional, such as a financial advisor, who can cause monetary harm to another may require ______ insurance.

A. malpractice; errors and omissions
B. errors and omissions; malpractice
C. malpractice; malpractice
D. errors and omissions; errors and omissions

13. Which of the following is an investment's rate of return without adjusting for inflation?

A. Real return
B. Nominal return
C. Coupon rate
D. Risk premium

14. Under the Social Security system, a fully insured worker is one that has paid into the system for at least _______ during his or her employment career.

A. 10 quarters
B. 20 quarters
C. 30 quarters
D. 40 quarters

15. The roles and responsibilities of FINRA include all but which of the following?

A. Writing and enforcing rules governing the ethical activities of all registered broker-dealer firms and registered brokers.
B. Maintaining fair, orderly, and efficient markets.
C. Examining firms for compliance with established regulatory rules.
D. Fostering market transparency and educating investors.

16. Which of the following refers to the first time a company offers its shares of stock to the general public?

A. IPO
B. LBO
C. ICO
D. OTC

17. Which of the following is a legal document that allows an individual to specify wishes about medical treatment and artificial life support under specific circumstances?

A. Power of attorney
B. Power of appointment
C. Living will
D. Will

18. Which of the following is the maximum exclusion of gain on the sale of a principal residence for married couples filing a joint tax return who owned the house and used it as a principal residence during at least 2 of the last 5 years before the date of sale?

A. $0
B. $125,000
C. $250,000
D. $500,000

19. Which of the following is an event that causes a loss, such as fire, lightning, smoke, or theft?

A. Liability
B. Risk
C. Hazard
D. Peril

20. Which of the following is an IRA-based plan that allows employers to make contributions toward their employees' retirement or toward their own if self-employed?

A. TSP
B. SEP
C. FSA
D. PSP

21. Which of the following is the speed and ease with which a security may be bought or sold?

A. Transferability
B. Liquidity
C. Marketability
D. Flexibility

For questions 22 – 26, determine if the form of property ownership is subject to probate. Use only one answer per blank. Answers may be used more than once or not at all.

A. Avoids probate
B. Goes to probate

22. ____ JTWROS between spouses

23. ____ JTWROS between non-spouses

24. ____ Tenancy in common

25. ____ Tenancy by entirety

26. ____ Community property

27. Which of the following is backed by the full faith and credit of the U.S. government?

A. Student Loan Marketing Association notes (Sallie Maes)
B. Federal Home Loan Mortgage Corporation debentures (Freddie Macs)
C. Federal National Mortgage Association certificates (Fannie Maes)
D. Government National Mortgage Association certificates (Ginnie Maes)

28. Which of the following is the correct formula used to calculate the amount of each fixed annuity payment that can be excluded from an annuitant's ordinary income?

A. Exclusion ratio = investment in contract / expected return
B. Exclusion ratio = expected return / investment in contract
C. Exclusion ratio = 1 – (investment in contract / expected return)
D. Exclusion ratio = 1 – (expected return / investment in contract)

29. The collateral that is generally required for an individual to take a loan from a life insurance policy is:

A. stocks or bonds owned by the insured.
B. the insured's primary residence.
C. the cash value of the policy itself.
D. the insured's future income or accounts receivable.

30. For health insurance continuation coverage, COBRA stands for:

A. Coverage Options and Benefits Reimbursement Act.
B. Consolidated Omnibus Budget Reconciliation Act.
C. Continuation of Benefits and Reimbursements Act.
D. Coverage Obligations and Benefits Reimbursement Act.

31. Jeremy owns an investment yielding an after-tax return of 5%. If he is in the 20% tax bracket, what is the equivalent pre-tax return?

A. 4.05%
B. 4.10%
C. 6.10%
D. 6.25%

32. A decedent is defined as a:

A. person who does not have a will.
B. person who has died.
C. person who inherits property.
D. person who has a trust.

33. A _______ tax structure takes a larger percentage of income from high-income earners than from low-income earners, and it is the tax structure used in the United States.

A. proportional
B. regressive
C. progressive
D. value-added

34. Which of the following refers to land and improvements to land?

A. Real property
B. Personal property
C. Community property
D. None of the above are correct.

35. The net worth statement is also referred to as which of the following?

A. Profit and loss statement
B. Balance sheet
C. Statement of retained earnings
D. Statement of changes in equity

36. Which of the following is a provision in an insurance policy that eliminates coverage for certain acts, property, types of damage, or locations?

A. Rider
B. Endorsement
C. Exclusion
D. Clause

37. All qualified retirement plans must satisfy the reporting and disclosure requirements as specified by:

A. TILA.
B. FACTA.
C. FCBA.
D. ERISA.

38. Which of the following is the cost of borrowing money?

A. Discount rate
B. Yield
C. Credit
D. Interest

39. Certain expenses, payments, contributions, and fees that can be subtracted from gross income to arrive at AGI are known as:

A. tax credits.
B. adjustments to income.
C. preference items.
D. tentative tax items.

40. Which of the following is the risk that bond prices will fall as interest rates rise?

A. Interest rate risk
B. Reinvestment risk
C. Purchase power risk
D. Market risk

41. With a ______ power of attorney, the agent's ability to act on behalf of the principal continues in the event of the principal's incapacity.

A. springing
B. durable
C. non-durable
D. limited

42. Which of the following is a type of credit score that lenders use to assess an individual's credit risk?

A. GAAP
B. FDIC
C. FICO
D. CAPM

43. Which of the following is the category of risk that will result in either loss or no loss without the possibility of financial gain?

A. Gambling
B. Pure risk
C. Speculative risk
D. Investment risk

44. For a SIMPLE IRA, the employer must match dollar for dollar the first ______ of compensation that eligible employees elect to defer, or the employer must make annual nonelective contributions equal to ______ of compensation for all eligible employees.

A. 2%; 3%
B. 2%; 4%
C. 3%; 2%
D. 4%; 3%

45. Which of the following are the two main types of counseling skills used by financial planners when advising clients?

A. Directive and nondirective
B. Verbal and nonverbal
C. Active and passive
D. Defensive and offensive

46. The duties of an executor include all but which of the following?

A. Identifying and collecting the assets of the estate.
B. Safeguarding assets pending distribution to beneficiaries.
C. Paying the debts owed by the estate.
D. Amending the will as needed when distributing property.

47. Which of the following is a type of individual retirement account that allows a working spouse to contribute to a non-earning spouse's retirement savings?

A. SIMPLE IRA
B. SEP IRA
C. Spousal IRA
D. None of the above are correct.

48. Which of the following Schedules of IRS Form 1040 is associated with the correct description?

A. Schedule A: Profit or Loss from Business
B. Schedule B: Itemized Deductions
C. Schedule C: Interest and Ordinary Dividends
D. Schedule D: Capital Gains and Losses

49. Which of the following is a cost-sharing mechanism in group insurance plans where the insured pays a specified dollar amount of incurred medical expenses and the insurer pays the remainder?

A. Indemnity
B. HMO
C. Copay
D. Surcharge

50. Casey earns an annual salary of $50,000 and contributes to his company's 401(k) plan. He contributes 6% of his income and receives a matching contribution equal to $0.50 per dollar on the first 6% of his pay. What is the employer's matching contribution?

A. $750
B. $1,500
C. $2,250
D. $3,000

51. The holding period of property inherited from a decedent is considered to be ______ in nature.

A. sometimes short-term
B. always short-term
C. sometimes long-term
D. always long-term

52. Which of the following is a type of emotional bias in behavioral finance that refers to an individual's tendency to make irrational financial decisions based on how he or she believes a certain product or service will reflect their values?

A. Affinity bias
B. Self-control bias
C. Status quo bias
D. Self-attribution bias

53. Which of the following are primary issuers of individual bonds?

(1) Local government
(2) U.S. government
(3) An agency of the U.S. government
(4) Corporations

A. (1) and (4) only
B. (1), (2), and (3) only
C. (2), (3), and (4) only
D. All of the above are correct.

54. All but which of the following are methods of risk management?

A. Risk avoidance
B. Risk exchange
C. Risk reduction
D. Risk transfer

55. What is the intrinsic value of a bond with a $1,000 face value, an 8% coupon, and 4 years until maturity? Comparable bonds are currently yielding 9.8%.

A. $941.60
B. $970.17
C. $1,000.00
D. $1,138.19

56. Which of the following type of life insurance is characterized by the insured paying a premium and receiving coverage for a specific number of years along with a fixed death benefit?

A. Universal life insurance
B. Variable life insurance
C. Survivorship life insurance
D. Term life insurance

57. Which of the following is considered a "pass-through entity" because it passes corporate income, losses, deductions, and credits through to shareholders for federal tax purposes?

A. REIT
B. C corporation
C. S corporation
D. None of the above are correct.

58. Which of the following is the concept that higher expected investment returns accompany greater risk, and vice versa?

A. Adjusted risk hypothesis
B. Risk-return tradeoff
C. PRIME risk theory
D. Opportunity cost principle

59. All but which of the following are correct regarding charitable contributions?

A. If a contribution entitles the donor to merchandise, goods, or services, the donor can only deduct the amount of the contribution that exceeds the fair market value of the benefits received.
B. A qualified appraisal is required for certain gifts.
C. Deductions for contributions of a donor's time or services are subject to AGI limits.
D. Charitable deductions that are disallowed due to AGI limits may be carried forward.

60. Which of the following is/are correct regarding survivorship life insurance policies?

(1) A survivorship life insurance policy results in a lower premium than a single life policy.
(2) A survivorship life insurance policy can be used to fund the payment of estate taxes at the second spouse's death.

A. (1) only
B. (2) only
C. None of the above are correct.
D. All of the above are correct.

61. Which of the following is a defined contribution plan that allows employees to participate in company profits through a plan formula established by the employer?

A. Pension plan
B. Cash balance plan
C. Defined benefit plan
D. None of the above are correct.

62. All but which of the following are correct regarding unsubsidized student loans?

A. They are loans for both undergraduate and graduate students.
B. Interest rates are federally regulated and subject to change.
C. They are based on financial need.
D. Interest begins to accrue immediately even though payments aren't due until after graduation.

63. Which of the following risks is associated with foreign currencies and their relationship with the U.S. dollar?

A. Credit risk
B. Exchange rate risk
C. Default risk
D. Market risk

64. For a traditional IRA, catch up contributions are permitted for individuals:

A. age 45 and younger.
B. age 45 and older.
C. age 50 and younger.
D. age 50 and older.

65. If money remains in a health savings account (HSA) at the end of the year, which of the following will occur?

A. The money will be forfeited.
B. The money will be carried over to the following year.
C. The money will be transferred to a traditional IRA.
D. The money will be converted to a Roth IRA.

66. Kelsey's annual gross income is $50,000. If she pays $15,000 in annual income tax, then her total consumer debt payments, such as credit cards and car loans, should not exceed _______ per month.

A. $583.33
B. $816.67
C. $833.33
D. $1,166.67

67. Which of the following investment strategies could be considered the opposite of diversification?

A. Multi-asset strategy
B. Concentrated portfolio
C. Balanced investing
D. Global allocation

68. Which of the following is a method for valuing an insured's home that uses the cost to rebuild or replace the structure with new property of like kind and quality, without subtracting depreciation?

A. Substitute cost value
B. Actual cash value
C. Replacement cost value
D. Depreciation cash value

69. A Roth IRA must be funded with which of the following?

A. Pre-tax dollars
B. Taxable dollars
C. Deferred dollars
D. After-tax dollars

70. All but which of the following are included as part of the fiduciary standard for financial planning professionals?

A. To provide full and adequate disclosure of all material facts.
B. To limit investment risk.
C. To expose all conflicts of interest.
D. To not mislead clients.

71. Which of the following generally will make a one-time public offering of only a specific, fixed number of securities or units like a closed-end fund? It will terminate and dissolve on a date that is specified at the time it's created.

A. Unit investment trust (UIT)
B. Guaranteed investment contract (GIC)
C. Initial public offering (IPO)
D. Master limited partnership (MLP)

72. Which of the following is the risk associated with a company's decision to use debt as part of its capital structure?

A. Financial risk
B. Market risk
C. Default risk
D. Interest rate risk

73. All but which of the following are examples of quantitative data?

A. Cash flow statement
B. Goals
C. Insurance coverage
D. Investment portfolio

74. **Amy's employer offers contributory group disability coverage to its employees. If she contributes 50% of the premium with after-tax dollars, and her disability benefit is $5,400 per month, what will be the tax consequences to Amy if she were to become disabled?**

A. $0 will be taxable, and $5,400 will be tax-free each month.
B. $1,350 will be taxable, and $4,050 will be tax-free each month.
C. $2,700 will be taxable, and $2,700 will be tax-free each month.
D. $5,400 will be taxable, and $0 will be tax-free each month.

75. **Which of the following is an investment strategy characterized by an investor purchasing securities with the intention of keeping them until maturity or for an extended period of time?**

A. Core-satellite strategy
B. Buy and hold strategy
C. Long-short strategy
D. Market timing strategy

ANSWER KEY

1. C
An interest-only mortgage allows a borrower to defer making principal payments for a set time, typically seven to ten years.

2. D
An A-trust (also referred to as a marital trust), B-trust (also referred to as a bypass trust or credit shelter trust), and C-trust (also referred to as a QTIP trust or current income trust) may be used to reduce estate taxes between married couples.

3. C
A $1,000 bond with a 4.5% coupon will pay a bondholder $45.00 per year.

4. B
REITs can be purchased in small denominations, and losses cannot be passed through to investors to deduct personally. REIT shareholders are not subject to double taxation.

5. A
An insurance agent represents the insurer, and a broker represents the customer.

6. D
In a SWOT analysis, the "O" stands for opportunities.

7. B
A nonelective contribution is a retirement plan contribution made by an employer for each eligible employee, regardless of whether the employee decides to make a salary deferral to the account.

8. C
Relating to the time value of money, an ordinary annuity is when a payment is made at the end of the period.

9. D
The efficient market hypothesis suggests that the stock market's efficiency in valuing securities is rapid and accurate. Therefore, investors are unable to outperform the stock market on a consistent basis, and any excess returns are temporary and will regress to the mean. According to the efficient market hypothesis, daily fluctuations in stock prices are a result of a random walk pattern and are not related to modern portfolio theory.

10. B
A future interest gift is a gift in which the donee's right to use, possess, and enjoy the property and income derived from the property does not begin until a future date.

11. C
For payments to qualify as alimony, the two parties cannot file a joint tax return or live together at the time of payment. The payments must be received for the benefit of the recipient and must be made in cash. Alimony payments cannot continue beyond the death of the recipient.

12. A
A professional, such as a physician, who can cause bodily harm to another, may require malpractice insurance. A professional, such as a financial advisor, who can cause monetary harm to another, may require errors and omissions insurance.

13. B
An investment's rate of return without adjusting for inflation is its nominal return.

14. D
Under the Social Security system, a fully insured worker is one that has paid into the system for at least 40 quarters during his or her employment career.

15. B
The roles and responsibilities of FINRA include writing and enforcing rules governing the ethical activities of all registered broker-dealer firms and registered brokers, examining firms for compliance with those rules, and fostering market transparency and educating investors. The SEC, not FINRA, is responsible for maintaining fair, orderly, and efficient markets.

16. A
IPO (initial public offering) refers to the first time a company offers its shares of stock to the general public.

17. C
A living will is a legal document that allows an individual to specify wishes about medical treatment and artificial life support under specific circumstances.

18. D
The maximum exclusion of gain on the sale of a principal residence for married couples filing a joint tax return who owned the house and used it as a principal residence during at least 2 of the last 5 years before the date of sale is $500,000.

19. D
A peril is an event that causes a loss, such as fire, lightning, smoke, or theft.

20. B
A SEP (simplified employee pension) is an IRA-based plan that allows employers to make contributions toward their employees' retirement or toward their own if self-employed.

21. C
Marketability is the speed and ease with which a security may be bought or sold.

22. A
JTWROS between spouses avoids probate.

23. A
JTWROS between non-spouses avoids probate.

24. B
Tenancy in common goes to probate.

25. A
Tenancy by entirety avoids probate.

26. B
Community property goes to probate.

27. D
Only Government National Mortgage Association certificates (Ginnie Maes) are backed by the full faith and credit of the U.S. government.

28. A
Exclusion ratio = investment in contract / expected return

29. C
The collateral that is generally required for an individual to take a loan from a life insurance policy is the cash value of the policy itself.

30. B
For health insurance continuation coverage, COBRA stands for Consolidated Omnibus Budget Reconciliation Act.

31. D
Pre-tax return = 0.05 / (1 – 0.2) = 6.25%

32. B
A decedent is a person who has died.

33. C
A progressive tax structure takes a larger percentage of income from high-income earners than from low-income earners, and it is the tax structure used in the United States.

34. A
Real property refers to land and improvements to land.

35. B
The net worth statement is also referred to as a balance sheet.

36. C
An exclusion is a provision in an insurance policy that eliminates coverage for certain acts, property, types of damage, or locations.

37. D
All qualified retirement plans must satisfy the reporting and disclosure requirements as specified by ERISA.

38. D
Interest is the cost of borrowing money.

39. B
Certain expenses, payments, contributions, and fees that can be subtracted from gross income to arrive at AGI are known as adjustments to income.

40. A
Interest rate risk is the risk that bond prices will fall as interest rates rise.

41. B
With a durable power of attorney, the agent's ability to act on behalf of the principal continues in the event of the principal's incapacity.

42. C
A FICO score is a type of credit score that lenders use to assess an individual's credit risk.

43. B
Pure risk is the category of risk that will result in either loss or no loss without the possibility of financial gain.

44. C
For a SIMPLE IRA, the employer must match dollar for dollar the first 3% of compensation that eligible employees elect to defer, or the employer must make annual nonelective contributions equal to 2% of compensation for all eligible employees.

45. A
The two main types of counseling skills used by financial planners when advising clients are directive and nondirective.

46. D
The duties of an executor include identifying and collecting the assets of the estate, safeguarding assets pending distribution to beneficiaries, and paying the debts owed by the estate. The executor is not permitted to amend the will.

47. C
A spousal IRA is a type of individual retirement account that allows a working spouse to contribute to a non-earning spouse's retirement savings.

48. D
The correct Schedules for IRS Form 1040 are Schedule A: Itemized Deductions, Schedule B: Interest and Ordinary Dividends, Schedule C: Profit or Loss from Business, and Schedule D: Capital Gains and Losses.

49. C
A copay is a cost-sharing mechanism in group insurance plans where the insured pays a specified dollar amount of incurred medical expenses and the insurer pays the remainder.

50. B
$\$50{,}000 \times \$0.50 \times 0.06 = \$1{,}500$

51. D
The holding period of property inherited from a decedent is considered to always be long-term in nature. This is true even if the decedent had acquired the property only one day before his or her date of death.

52. A
Affinity bias is a type of emotional bias in behavioral finance that refers to an individual's tendency to make irrational financial decisions based on how he or she believes a certain product or service will reflect their values.

53. D
The primary issuers of individual bonds are local government, state government, U.S. government, an agency of the U.S. government, and corporations.

54. B
The methods of risk management are risk avoidance, risk reduction, risk retention, and risk transfer.

55. A
FV = $1,000
i = 9.8 / 2 = 4.9
n = 4 × 2 = 8
PMT = $1,000 × 0.08 = $80, then $80 / 2 = $40
PV = ? = $941.60

56. D
Term life insurance is characterized by the insured paying a premium and receiving coverage for a specific number of years along with a fixed death benefit.

57. C
An S corporation is considered a "pass-through entity" because it passes corporate income, losses, deductions, and credits through to shareholders for federal tax purposes. Shareholders report the flow-through of income and losses on their personal tax returns and must pay tax at their individual tax rates.

58. B
Risk-return tradeoff is the concept that higher expected investment returns accompany greater risk, and vice versa.

59. C
If a contribution entitles the donor to merchandise, goods, or services, the donor can only deduct the amount of the contribution that exceeds the fair market value of the benefits received. A qualified appraisal is required for certain gifts. Charitable deductions that are disallowed due to AGI limits may be carried forward. No deduction is allowed for a donor's contribution of time or services.

60. D
A survivorship life insurance policy results in a lower premium than a single life policy. The policy can be used to fund the payment of estate taxes at the second spouse's death.

61. D
A profit sharing plan is a defined contribution plan that allows employees to participate in company profits through a plan formula established by the employer.

62. C
Unsubsidized student loans are for both undergraduate and graduate students, and interest rates are federally regulated and subject to change. The interest begins to accrue immediately even though payments aren't due until after graduation. They are not based on financial need.

63. B
Exchange rate risk is associated with foreign currencies and their relationship with the U.S. dollar. It is the risk that an investment's value will change due to currency exchange rates.

64. D
For a traditional IRA, catch up contributions are permitted for individuals age 50 and older.

65. B
If money remains in a health savings account (HSA) at the end of the year, the money will be carried over to the following year.

66. A
Step 1: Net income = $50,000 – $15,000 = $35,000
Step 2: Maximum annual consumer debt = $35,000 × 0.2 = $7,000
Step 3: Maximum monthly consumer debt = $7,000 / 12 months = $583.33
Consumer debt payments, such as credit cards and car loans, should not exceed 20% of net income.

67. B
The investment strategy that could be considered the opposite of diversification is concentration or a concentrated portfolio.

68. C
Replacement cost value is a method for valuing an insured's home that uses the cost to rebuild or replace the structure with new property of like kind and quality, without subtracting depreciation.

69. D
A Roth IRA must be funded with after-tax dollars.

70. B
The fiduciary standard for financial planning professionals includes providing full and adequate disclosure of all material facts, exposing all conflicts of interest, and not misleading clients. Limiting investment risk is not part of the fiduciary standard, as clients may want to increase investment risk to achieve higher returns.

71. A
A unit investment trust (UIT) generally will make a one-time public offering of only a specific, fixed number of securities or units like a closed-end fund. It will terminate and dissolve on a date that is specified at the time it's created.

72. A
Financial risk is the risk associated with a company's decision to use debt as part of its capital structure.

73. B
The cash flow statement, insurance coverage, and investment portfolio are quantitative data. Goals are qualitative data.

74. C
$5,400 × 0.5 = $2,700
Because Amy is paying 50% of the premium with after-tax dollars, 50% of the benefits will be tax-free, and the other 50% will be taxable.

75. B
The buy and hold investment strategy is characterized by an investor purchasing securities with the intention of keeping them until maturity or for an extended period of time.

PRACTICE EXAM 10

QUESTIONS

1. Which of the following is a form of investment analysis that uses price data and volume data, typically displayed graphically in charts? The charts are analyzed using various indicators to make investment recommendations.

A. Fundamental analysis
B. Technical analysis
C. Contrarian analysis
D. Qualitative analysis

2. Kevin's son recently got his driver's license when he turned age 16. As a gift, Kevin bought his son a 20-year-old used car with 150,000 miles on it, for a cost of $2,000. Kevin purchased liability insurance, but no damage protection for the vehicle. Which method of risk management is Kevin using to deal with any potential damage that may occur to the car?

A. Reduction
B. Transfer
C. Avoidance
D. Retention

3. Which of the following is the legal concept that an injured party may receive compensation for damages even if he or she was partially responsible for causing the accident?

A. Comparative negligence
B. Contributory negligence
C. Strict liability
D. Vicarious liability

4. Which of the following standards is lower than a fiduciary duty and requires only that a broker has a reasonable basis to believe a recommended course of action is suitable for the client based on a reasonable inquiry into the client's investment profile?

A. Reasonability standard
B. Fiduciary standard
C. Broker standard
D. Suitability standard

5. To keep up with inflation, Social Security benefits are adjusted through:

A. AIMEs.
B. DOLPs.
C. COLAs.
D. ROICs.

6. Chapter 7 bankruptcy involves ______ of assets. Chapter 13 bankruptcy involves ______ of debt.

A. reorganization; liquidation
B. liquidation; reorganization
C. reorganization; reorganization
D. liquidation; liquidation

7. If an investor is using dollar cost averaging to purchase shares of stock over a 6-month period, which of the following would occur if the stock price were to rise throughout the period?

A. The investor would have maximized gains compared to all other investment methods.
B. The investor would have minimized gains compared to all other investment methods.
C. The investor would have missed out on potential gains compared to lump sum investing at the beginning of the period.
D. The investor would have missed out on potential gains compared to lump sum investing at the end of the period.

8. Which of the following is the amount of money that one person may transfer to another each year as a gift without incurring a gift tax or affecting the unified credit amount?

A. Transfer tax annual exemption
B. Charitable tax exclusion
C. Donor tax exemption
D. Gift tax annual exclusion

9. With which of the following vesting schedules will an employee's vested percentage in employer contributions start at less than 100% and increase with each year of service?

A. Graded vesting
B. Cliff vesting
C. Deferred vesting
D. Annual vesting

10. To be legally effective, all trusts must have which of the following?

(1) Grantor
(2) Trustee
(3) Corpus
(4) Beneficiary

A. (1) and (2) only
B. (1) and (3) only
C. (1), (2), and (4) only
D. None of the above are correct.

11. Thomas obtained a loan in the amount of $592,300. If the annual interest rate is 4.625%, then how much interest will he owe in the first year?

A. $2,282.82
B. $19,210.83
C. $26,482.34
D. $27,393.88

12. Gathering quantitative and qualitative information about the client is included in which step of the financial planning process?

A. Analyzing the client's current course of action and potential alternate courses of action.
B. Understanding the client's personal and financial circumstances.
C. Monitoring progress and updating.
D. Developing the financial planning recommendations.

13. Which of the following is a type of stock whose earnings are expected to increase at an above-average rate relative to the overall market?

A. Value stock
B. Growth stock
C. Global stock
D. International stock

14. Which of the following is/are correct regarding the alternative minimum tax (AMT)?

(1) A taxpayer will owe AMT if taxable income plus AMT adjustments and preference items exceed the AMT exemption amount.
(2) AMT tax brackets are the same as federal income tax brackets.

A. (1) only
B. (2) only
C. None of the above are correct.
D. All of the above are correct.

15. All but which of the following are life insurance non-forfeiture options?

A. Cash
B. Extended term
C. Paid-up reduced amount
D. Period certain and life

16. The "NAV" of a mutual fund is its:

A. nominal asset value.
B. net appreciation value.
C. net asset value.
D. nominal adjusted value.

17. Which of the following will result if a distribution is taken from a health savings account (HSA) by an individual under age 65, and the distribution is not used to pay for qualified medical expenses?

A. The distribution is subject to ordinary income tax only.
B. The distribution is subject to ordinary income tax and a 10% penalty.
C. The distribution is subject to ordinary income tax and a 20% penalty.
D. None of the above are correct.

18. Which of the following mortgages is characterized by having monthly payments that are generally not large enough to pay off the entire loan balance during the amortization period?

A. Graduated payment mortgage
B. Balloon mortgage
C. Fixed-rate mortgage
D. Adjustable-rate mortgage

19. Profit sharing plans have which of the following characteristics?

A. Loans may be permitted.
B. They favor older employees compared to defined benefit plans.
C. They are a type of defined contribution pension plan.
D. Employers are required to make annual contributions.

20. With the tenancy in common form of property ownership, which of the following occurs when one owner dies?

A. The decedent's share is distributed according to the provisions of the will, and the property avoids probate.
B. The decedent's share is distributed according to the provisions of the will, and the property is subject to probate.
C. The decedent's share bypasses the will when distributed, and the property is subject to probate.
D. The decedent's share bypasses the will when distributed, and the property avoids probate.

21. Which of the following establishes the order in which insurance plans pay their claims, and permits secondary plans to reduce their benefits so that the combined benefits from all plans doesn't exceed the total allowable expenses?

A. Subrogation clause
B. Collateral source rule
C. Adhesion clause
D. Coordination of benefits

22. All but which of the following are characteristics of a SIMPLE IRA?

A. Elective salary deferrals are made with after-tax dollars and are included in an employee's taxable income.
B. Employers are required to make matching or nonelective contributions.
C. Contributions and investment earnings grow tax-free until distributed.
D. The annual contribution limit for a SIMPLE IRA is generally higher than the limit for a traditional IRA.

23. Municipal bonds are generally issued by which of the following?

A. U.S. Treasury
B. State and local governments
C. Domestic corporations
D. Foreign countries

24. Which of the following is the rate of interest that is calculated on both the amount of money invested and the interest that has been added to it?

A. Simple rate
B. Compound rate
C. Arithmetic rate
D. Geometric rate

25. All but which of the following will receive a step-up in basis at death?

A. Real estate
B. Artwork
C. Common stock
D. 401(k) plan

26. Assuming semiannual compounding, what is the current price of a zero-coupon bond with a $1,000 face value, a yield to maturity of 7.98%, and 4 years until maturity?

A. $710.27
B. $719.78
C. $725.53
D. $731.25

27. Schedule B of IRS Form 1040 is used to report which of the following?

A. Capital gains and losses
B. Interest and ordinary dividends
C. Itemized deductions
D. Profit or loss from business

28. Which of the following is/are correct regarding the capital structure of open-end mutual funds?

(1) Open-end mutual funds issue new shares and redeem existing shares from shareholders.
(2) The price an investor pays when buying shares of an open-end mutual fund is based on supply and demand.

A. (1) only
B. (2) only
C. None of the above are correct.
D. All of the above are correct.

29. Which of the following describes speculative risk?

A. Risk that results in only an uncertain degree of loss.
B. Risk that results in an uncertain degree of gain or loss.
C. Risk that results in an opportunity to break even or achieve an uncertain degree of gain.
D. None of the above are correct.

30. A living trust is also known as which of the following?

A. Ad valorem trust
B. De novo trust
C. Inter vivos trust
D. Ad litem trust

31. Which of the following is/are correct regarding insurance provided by the PBGC?

(1) The PBGC provides mandatory insurance for defined benefit plans.
(2) The PBGC insures all pension plans, but not profit sharing plans.

A. (1) only
B. (2) only
C. None of the above are correct.
D. All of the above are correct.

32. All but which of the following are among the five C's of credit that a lender considers when evaluating a borrower?

A. Capacity
B. Credit score
C. Collateral
D. Conditions

33. Which of the following will generally occur if an individual's gross income exceeds the standard deduction?

A. The individual will be required to file a federal income tax return.
B. The individual will not need to file a federal income tax return.
C. The individual will need to file an amended federal income tax return.
D. The individual will receive a federal income tax refund.

34. In which of the following circumstances will a standard power of attorney lapse?

A. When the principal dies.
B. When the agent dies.
C. When the principal becomes mentally incapacitated.
D. All of the above are correct.

35. Longevity risk is a type of:

A. credit risk.
B. business risk.
C. unsystematic risk.
D. systematic risk.

36. Which of the following definitions of disability is most favorable to the insured and least favorable to the insurer?

A. Any occupation
B. Split definition
C. Modified own occupation
D. Own occupation

37. Which of the following is a fixed income investment that represents a loan made by an investor to a borrower (issuer)?

A. Bond
B. Money market fund
C. Annuity
D. Preferred stock

38. Which of the following is a defined benefit plan that defines each employee's benefit in terms of a stated account balance, similar to a defined contribution plan?

A. Cash balance plan
B. Thrift savings plan
C. Money purchase pension plan
D. Employee stock ownership plan

39. The cash flow statement shows which of the following?

A. Assets and liabilities
B. Money inflows and outflows
C. Income and expenses
D. All of the above are correct.

40. Purchasing power risk is most closely related to which of the following?

A. Rising prices
B. Credit quality
C. Default risk
D. Bond values

41. In estate planning, portability of the ______ allows the surviving spouse to potentially reduce or eliminate federal estate taxes due.

A. GRAT
B. QPRT
C. DSUE
D. ILIT

42. Which of the following is correct regarding an individual who fails to meet the material participation standard for a trade or business activity?

A. No losses can be deducted.
B. All losses can be deducted.
C. Any losses from the activity are considered passive and can only be deducted to the extent of passive income.
D. Any losses from the activity are considered active and can only be deducted to the extent of active income.

43. An automatic premium loan provision may be available for which of the following type of insurance?

A. Term life insurance
B. Disability insurance
C. Long-term care insurance
D. Permanent life insurance

44. Associated with retirement planning, an RMD is a:

A. required market disclosure.
B. retirement maximum distribution.
C. risk management disclosure.
D. required minimum distribution.

45. Which of the following Acts requires prompt written acknowledgment of consumer billing complaints and investigation of billing errors by creditors and prohibits creditors from taking actions that adversely affect a consumer's credit standing until an investigation is completed?

A. Truth in Lending Act (TILA)
B. Fair Credit Billing Act (FCBA)
C. Fair and Accurate Credit Transactions Act (FACTA)
D. Equal Credit Opportunity Act (ECOA)

46. Which of the following is/are correct regarding beta?

(1) Beta is used to measure the amount of unsystematic risk in an investor's portfolio.
(2) A portfolio's beta can be positive or equal to zero, but cannot be negative.

A. (1) only
B. (2) only
C. None of the above are correct.
D. All of the above are correct.

47. All but which of the following can serve as a will substitute?

A. Property held as a sole proprietorship.
B. Property held tenancy by entirety.
C. Retirement plan beneficiary designation.
D. Life insurance policy beneficiary designation.

48. Which of the following is a consumption tax on the exchange of goods or services that is paid by the consumer and imposed by state or local governments?

A. Property tax
B. Income tax
C. Sales tax
D. Capital gains tax

49. Which of the following assets are correctly ranked from most liquid to least liquid?

(1) Real estate
(2) Treasury bills
(3) Limited partnership
(4) High-grade corporate bonds

A. 2, 1, 4, 3
B. 4, 2, 3, 1
C. 3, 1, 4, 2
D. 2, 4, 1, 3

50. Which of the following is a limitation in an insurance policy on the amount of coverage available to cover a specific type of loss?

A. Coinsurance
B. Sublimit
C. Deductible
D. Stop-loss

51. All but which of the following are correct regarding a bond's par value?

A. It can also be referred to as the bond's face value.
B. A common par value for a bond is $1,000.
C. It is always equal to the market value of the bond.
D. All of the above are correct.

52. Which of the following is a student loan available to the parent of an undergraduate student to pay for qualified education expenses?

A. HEAL loan
B. PLUS loan
C. FELP loan
D. STIP loan

53. Which of the following is a right to name a representative to receive a beneficial interest in property?

A. Power of appointment
B. Advance directive
C. Bequest
D. Devise

54. Which of the following is total income from all sources, and is the starting point for calculating other types of income such as AGI?

A. Revenue
B. Gross profit
C. Gross income
D. Net income

55. Which of the following provides additional liability coverage beyond the standard limits available through home and automobile insurance policies?

A. Credit insurance
B. Professional liability insurance
C. Cyber insurance
D. Umbrella insurance

56. Which of the following is/are correct regarding certificates of deposit (CDs)?

(1) CDs are known as "time deposits."
(2) CDs generally pay variable rates of interest.

A. (1) only
B. (2) only
C. None of the above are correct.
D. All of the above are correct.

57. All but which of the following accounts allow catch up contributions?

A. 401(k), 403(b), and 457 accounts
B. Roth and traditional IRAs
C. Health savings accounts
D. All of the above are correct.

58. Market risk is a type of:

A. unsystematic risk.
B. systematic risk.
C. volatility risk.
D. event risk.

59. Which of the following is correct regarding property disclaimed by a beneficiary (disclaimant)?

A. A disclaimant may direct how disclaimed property is to be distributed under certain circumstances.
B. A disclaimant may not direct how disclaimed property is to be distributed.
C. A disclaimant is responsible for paying gift taxes owed on disclaimed property.
D. A disclaimant is responsible for paying estate taxes owed on disclaimed property.

60. Which of the following can be used by a homeowner to borrow against the equity in his or her home?

A. PLOC
B. PMI
C. HELOC
D. APR

61. Which of the following is a type of hazard that deals with negligence or carelessness?

A. Moral
B. Morale
C. Physical
D. Negligent

62. Which of the following is a defined contribution plan designed to provide benefits similar to those of a profit sharing plan, except that benefits are distributed to employees in the form of stock rather than cash?

A. Stock bonus plan
B. Employee stock purchase plan
C. Cash balance plan
D. Target benefit plan

63. Copyrights, patents, licenses, and trademarks are examples of:

A. business realty.
B. business commodities.
C. intangible property.
D. intangible commodities.

64. Which of the following is/are correct regarding gifts of a future interest?

(1) They are eligible for the gift tax annual exclusion.
(2) They include gifts of a remainder and reversionary interest.

A. (1) only
B. (2) only
C. None of the above are correct.
D. All of the above are correct.

65. Which of the following is a type of bond that has no reinvestment risk?

A. Floating-rate bond
B. High-yield bond
C. Inflation-indexed bond
D. Zero-coupon bond

66. Which of the following is correct regarding the comparison between education grants and education loans?

A. Both grants and loans must be repaid.
B. Neither grants nor loans need to be repaid.
C. Grants do not need to be repaid, while loans must be repaid.
D. Grants must be repaid, while loans do not need to be repaid.

67. All but which of the following are characteristics of an LLC?

A. Majority approval is required to transfer management rights.
B. It provides limited liability to all members.
C. An operating agreement is not required.
D. It provides pass-through taxation.

68. Which of the following is a written contract between an individual and an insurance company in which the insurance company promises to make a series of payments in exchange for a single premium or multiple premiums paid?

A. Unit investment trust
B. Certificate of deposit
C. Annuity
D. None of the above are correct.

69. A bond with a $1,000 face value has a current yield of 4.25%. If the bond pays a 4% coupon payment, what is the market price of the bond?

A. $941.18
B. $966.49
C. $1,058.82
D. $1,084.26

The following information relates to questions 70 – 71.

Max owns a whole life insurance policy with a waiver of premium rider. The monthly premium is $400 and the death benefit is $750,000. Max is in the 25% tax bracket.

70. If Max were to become disabled, the insurer would pay ______ of the premium.

A. 0%
B. 25%
C. 50%
D. 100%

71. If Max were to die, the death benefit would be taxed at a rate of:

A. 0%.
B. 25%.
C. 75%.
D. 100%.

72. Which of the following is/are correct if a fiduciary fails to meet the standards of conduct in a qualified retirement plan?

(1) The fiduciary may be held personally liable for losses incurred by the plan.
(2) The fiduciary may be subject to civil and criminal actions.

A. (1) only
B. (2) only
C. None of the above are correct.
D. All of the above are correct.

73. Which of the following provisions allows a bond to be redeemed by the issuer at a predetermined time before its listed maturity date?

A. Subordination provision
B. Call provision
C. Conversion provision
D. Collateral provision

74. Which of the following plans would be most likely to calculate a participant's benefit through a plan formula that considers such factors as salary and service years? For example, 1% of average salary for the last 3 years of employment for every year of service with an employer.

A. Defined benefit plan
B. SIMPLE IRA
C. 401(k) plan
D. Roth IRA

75. All but which of the following are correct regarding matching contributions in a retirement plan?

A. They are additional contributions made by employers on top of the contributions made by employees.
B. They are typically made on a percentage basis, such as 25%, 50%, or 100% of the employee's contribution amount, up to certain limits.
C. They are generally immediately vested.
D. All of the above are correct.

ANSWER KEY

1. B
Technical analysis is a form of investment analysis that uses price data and volume data, typically displayed graphically in charts. The charts are analyzed using various indicators to make investment recommendations.

2. D
By not purchasing damage protection for the car, Kevin is retaining the risk.

3. A
Comparative negligence is the legal concept that an injured party may receive compensation for damages even if he or she was partially responsible for causing the accident.

4. D
The suitability standard is lower than a fiduciary duty and requires only that a broker has a reasonable basis to believe a recommended course of action is suitable for the client based on a reasonable inquiry into the client's investment profile.

5. C
To keep up with inflation, Social Security benefits are adjusted through COLAs (cost of living adjustments).

6. B
Chapter 7 bankruptcy involves liquidation of assets. Chapter 13 bankruptcy involves reorganization of debt.

7. C
If an investor is using dollar cost averaging to purchase shares of stock over a 6-month period, and the stock price were to rise throughout the period, the investor would have missed out on potential gains compared to lump sum investing at the beginning of the period.

8. D
The gift tax annual exclusion is the amount of money that one person may transfer to another each year as a gift without incurring a gift tax or affecting the unified credit amount.

9. A
With a graded vesting schedule, an employee's vested percentage in employer contributions starts at less than 100% and increases with each year of service.

10. C
To be legally effective, all trusts must have a grantor, trustee, and beneficiary.

11. D
Annual interest = $592,300 × 0.04625 = $27,393.88

12. B
Gathering quantitative and qualitative information about the client is included in the first step of the financial planning process, which is "understanding the client's personal and financial circumstances."

13. B
Growth stocks are characterized by having earnings that are expected to increase at an above-average rate relative to the overall market.

14. A
A taxpayer will owe AMT if taxable income plus AMT adjustments and preference items exceed the AMT exemption amount. AMT tax brackets are different than the federal income tax brackets.

15. D
Life insurance non-forfeiture options include cash, extended term, and paid-up reduced amount.

16. C
The "NAV" of a mutual fund is its net asset value.

17. C
Distributions from a health savings account (HSA) that are not used to pay for qualified medical expenses are subject to ordinary income tax and a 20% penalty. The penalty is waived if the individual is age 65 or older.

18. B
A balloon mortgage is characterized by having monthly payments that are generally not large enough to pay off the entire loan balance during the amortization period.

19. A
Profit sharing plans tend to favor younger employees, and loans may be permitted. Profit sharing plans are a type of defined contribution plan other than a pension plan. Their contributions must be substantial and recurring, but are not required annually.

20. B
With the tenancy in common form of property ownership, when one owner dies, his or her share is distributed according to the provisions of the will, and the property is subject to probate.

21. D
Coordination of benefits establishes the order in which insurance plans pay their claims and permits secondary plans to reduce their benefits so that the combined benefits from all plans doesn't exceed the total allowable expenses.

22. A
Elective salary deferrals for a SIMPLE IRA are made with pre-tax dollars and are excluded from an employee's taxable income. Employers are required to make matching or nonelective contributions. Contributions and investment earnings grow tax-free until distributed. The annual contribution limit for a SIMPLE IRA is generally higher than the limit for a traditional IRA.

23. B
Municipal bonds are generally issued by state and local governments.

24. B
The compound rate is the rate of interest that is calculated on both the amount of money invested and the interest that has been added to it.

25. D
Of the items listed, real estate, artwork, and common stock will receive a step-up in basis at death. A 401(k) plan does not receive a step-up in basis at death because it is a tax-deferred retirement account.

26. D
FV = $1,000
n = 4 × 2 = 8
i = 7.98 / 2 = 3.99
PMT = 0
PV = ? = $731.25

27. B
Schedule B of IRS Form 1040 is used to report interest and ordinary dividends.

28. A
Open-end mutual funds issue new shares and redeem existing shares from shareholders. The price an investor pays when buying shares of an open-end mutual fund is based on the fund's net asset value (NAV).

29. B
Speculative risk results in an uncertain degree of gain or loss.

30. C
A living trust is also known as an inter vivos trust.

31. A
The PBGC (Pension Benefit Guaranty Corporation) provides mandatory insurance for defined benefit plans only. It does not insure all pension plans, because some pension plans are defined contribution plans.

32. B
The five C's of credit that a lender considers when evaluating a borrower are character, capital, capacity, collateral, and conditions.

33. A
If an individual's gross income exceeds the standard deduction, then he or she will generally be required to file a federal income tax return.

34. D
A standard power of attorney lapses when the principal or agent dies, or when the principal becomes mentally incapacitated.

35. C
Longevity risk is a type of unsystematic risk.

36. D
The "own occupation" definition of disability is most favorable to the insured and least favorable to the insurer because it contains the broadest definition of disability.

37. A
A bond is a fixed income investment that represents a loan made by an investor to a borrower (issuer).

38. A
A cash balance plan is a defined benefit plan that defines each employee's benefit in terms of a stated account balance, similar to a defined contribution plan.

39. B
The cash flow statement shows money inflows and outflows.

40. A
Purchasing power risk is most closely related to rising prices (inflation).

41. C
In estate planning, portability of the DSUE (deceased spousal unused exclusion) allows the surviving spouse to potentially reduce or eliminate federal estate taxes due.

42. C
If an individual fails to meet the material participation standard for a trade or business activity, then any losses from the activity are considered passive and can only be deducted to the extent of passive income.

43. D
An automatic premium loan provision may be available for permanent life insurance.

44. D
Associated with retirement planning, an RMD is a required minimum distribution.

45. B
The Fair Credit Billing Act (FCBA) requires prompt written acknowledgment of consumer billing complaints and investigation of billing errors by creditors and prohibits creditors from taking actions that adversely affect a consumer's credit standing until an investigation is completed.

46. C
Beta is used to measure the amount of systematic risk in an investor's portfolio. A portfolio's beta can be positive, negative, or equal to zero.

47. A
Property held tenancy by entirety, retirement plan beneficiary designations, and life insurance policy beneficiary designations can serve as will substitutes. Property held as a sole proprietorship is subject to probate and does not serve as a will substitute.

48. C
Sales tax is a consumption tax on the exchange of goods or services that is paid by the consumer and imposed by state or local governments.

49. D
The assets ranked from most liquid to least liquid are Treasury bills, high-grade corporate bonds, real estate, and the limited partnership.

50. B
A sublimit is a limitation in an insurance policy on the amount of coverage available to cover a specific type of loss.

51. C
A bond's par value can also be referred to as its face value, and it may be different than the market value of the bond. A common par value is $1,000.

52. B
A PLUS loan (parent loan for undergraduate students) is a student loan available to the parent of an undergraduate student to pay for qualified education expenses.

53. A
A power of appointment is a right to name a representative to receive a beneficial interest in property.

54. C
Gross income is total income from all sources and is the starting point for calculating other types of income such as AGI.

55. D
Umbrella insurance provides additional liability coverage beyond the standard limits available through home and automobile policies.

56. A
CDs are known as "time deposits" and they generally pay fixed rates of interest.

57. D
401(k), 403(b), 457 accounts, Roth and traditional IRAs, and health savings accounts allow catch up contributions.

58. B
Market risk is a type of systematic risk.

59. B
A disclaimant may not direct how disclaimed property is to be distributed. It must pass according to the transferor's directions.

60. C
A HELOC (home equity line of credit) can be used by a homeowner to borrow against the equity in his or her home.

61. B
Morale hazard deals with negligence or carelessness.

62. A
A stock bonus plan is a defined contribution plan designed to provide benefits similar to those of a profit sharing plan, except that benefits are distributed to employees in the form of stock rather than cash.

63. C
Copyrights, patents, licenses, and trademarks are examples of intangible property.

64. B
Gifts of a future interest are not eligible for the gift tax annual exclusion. They include gifts of a remainder and reversionary interest.

65. D
A zero-coupon bond is a type of bond that has no reinvestment risk.

66. C
Education grants do not need to be repaid, while education loans must be repaid.

67. C
An LLC provides limited liability and pass-through taxation to all members. Majority approval is required to transfer management rights, and an operating agreement is required to determine the management structure.

68. C
An annuity is a written contract between an individual and an insurance company in which the insurance company promises to make a series of payments in exchange for a single premium or multiple premiums paid.

69. A
Current yield = sum of coupon payments / market price
0.0425 = $40 / market price
Market price = $941.18

70. D
Because Max owns a whole life insurance policy that includes a waiver of premium rider, if he were to become disabled, the insurer would pay 100% of the premium.

71. A
Max would not owe any tax because the death benefit from a life insurance policy is not taxable.

72. D
A fiduciary who fails to meet the standards of conduct in a qualified retirement plan may be held personally liable for losses incurred by the plan and may be subject to civil and criminal actions.

73. B
A call provision allows a bond to be redeemed by the issuer at a predetermined time before its listed maturity date.

74. A
Of the options provided, a defined benefit plan would be most likely to calculate a participant's benefit through a plan formula that considers such factors as salary and service years. For example, 1% of average salary for the last 3 years of employment for every year of service with an employer.

75. C
Matching contributions are additional contributions made by employers on top of the contributions made by employees. They are typically made on a percentage basis, such as 25%, 50%, or 100% of the employee's contribution amount, up to certain limits. Matching contributions generally are not immediately vested.

PRACTICE EXAM 11

QUESTIONS

1. Which of the following is a bond that is sold at a deep discount from face value and does not pay interest prior to maturity?

A. Floating rate bond
B. Callable bond
C. Zero-coupon bond
D. General obligation bond

2. All but which of the following are major credit bureaus in the United States?

A. Equifax
B. Altruist
C. Experian
D. TransUnion

3. With a _______ power of attorney, the agent's ability to act on behalf of the principal stops in the event of the principal's incapacity.

A. non-durable
B. durable
C. springing
D. living

4. Which of the following is a life insurance policy that pays a dividend?

A. Participating policy
B. Non-participating policy
C. Noncancellable policy
D. Waiver of premium policy

5. Which of the following provides deposit insurance to protect customer money in the event of a bank failure?

A. PBGC
B. CFPB
C. NCUA
D. FDIC

6. A mutual fund that invests only in securities outside the U.S. is a/an:

A. balanced fund.
B. international fund.
C. global fund.
D. aggressive growth fund.

7. Which of the following is/are correct regarding a bond's yield to maturity?

(1) Higher risk bonds have lower yields to maturity.
(2) If a bond's coupon rate is greater than its yield to maturity, the bond will sell at a premium.

A. (1) only
B. (2) only
C. None of the above are correct.
D. All of the above are correct.

8. Which of the following is a legal document that coordinates the distribution of probate property after death and can appoint guardians for minor children?

A. Will
B. Power of appointment
C. Power of attorney
D. Advance directive

9. Which of the following requirements must be met for a donor to make an inter vivos gift?

(1) The donor must be legally competent.
(2) The donee must be capable of receiving and possessing the property.
(3) There must be delivery to, and acceptance by, the donee or the donee's agent.
(4) The donor must make a "complete" gift.

A. (1) and (3) only
B. (2) and (4) only
C. (1), (2), and (3) only
D. All of the above are correct.

10. Which of the following is the principal amount that an investor will be paid upon maturity of a bond?

A. Coupon value
B. Par value
C. Present value
D. Future value

11. Which of the following is a type of retirement plan in which only the employer contributes money toward the retirement benefits of the employees?

A. Noncontributory pension plan
B. Contributory profit sharing plan
C. Defined contribution plan
D. None of the above are correct.

12. For a qualified retirement plan, a fiduciary under the provisions of ERISA is an individual who meets which of the following criteria?

(1) Has discretionary authority or responsibility over plan administration.
(2) Exercises discretionary authority over plan management.
(3) Provides investment advice for a fee or other compensation.
(4) Exercises authority or control over the disposition of plan assets.

A. (1) and (3) only
B. (2) and (4) only
C. (1), (2), and (4) only
D. All of the above are correct.

13. Which of the following is a sales charge that may be imposed when an investor purchases mutual fund shares through an investment company?

A. Tax
B. Load
C. Rate
D. Yield

14. Dawn has a 401(k) plan and named her brother, Rich, as the sole beneficiary several years ago. However, Dawn has recently decided that she'd instead like to pass her 401(k) to her sister, Lisa, at death. Dawn has not updated her 401(k) beneficiary designation, but she has drafted a will that states that she wants the 401(k) to pass to Lisa. What will be the result when Dawn dies?

A. The 401(k) will pass to Rich because the beneficiary designation bypasses the will.
B. The 401(k) will pass to Lisa because the will supersedes the beneficiary designation.
C. The 401(k) will be split between Rich and Lisa.
D. The 401(k) will pass through probate because the will and beneficiary designation are different.

For questions 15 – 18, choose the correct tax treatment for the items listed. Use only one answer per blank. Answers may be used more than once or not at all.

A. Included in income
B. Excluded from income

15. ____ **Unemployment compensation**

16. ____ **Military combat pay**

17. ____ **Prizes**

18. ____ **Tips and gratuities**

19. Which of the following is a common exclusion from a homeowners insurance policy?

A. Fire
B. Lightning
C. Flood
D. Theft

20. Business risk is a type of:

A. interest rate risk.
B. market risk.
C. systematic risk.
D. unsystematic risk.

21. Which of the following is the maximum percentage of Social Security benefits that may be subject to tax?

A. 0%
B. 50%
C. 85%
D. 100%

22. Which of the following involves reinvesting an investment's earnings so that it produces additional gains over time?

A. Annuitizing
B. Compounding
C. Discounting
D. Yielding

23. Common stock is referred to as _______ because the owner of the stock is also an owner of the corporation and may participate in its capital and income growth.

A. convertible stock
B. preferred stock
C. debt
D. equity

24. Which of the following is the correct formula to calculate the adjusted basis of an asset?

A. Adjusted basis = cost – expenses of sale + depreciation
B. Adjusted basis = cost + expenses of sale + depreciation
C. Adjusted basis = cost + expenses of sale – depreciation
D. Adjusted basis = cost – expenses of sale – depreciation

25. Which of the following lines of insurance are needed for a retiring 58-year-old client who has a good defined benefit plan at her current job?

(1) Long-term care insurance
(2) Life insurance
(3) Disability insurance
(4) Health insurance

A. (1) and (3) only
B. (1) and (4) only
C. (2) and (3) only
D. All of the above are correct.

26. A graduated payment mortgage is characterized by which of the following?

A. Payments start large and decrease over the life of the mortgage.
B. Payments start small and increase over the life of the mortgage.
C. The interest rate starts high and decreases over the life of the mortgage.
D. The interest rate starts low and increases over the life of the mortgage.

27. Within the Social Security system, which of the following is used to calculate a worker's primary insurance amount?

A. OASDI
B. SSI
C. AIME
D. PIA

28. The standard deviation of an investment portfolio must be _______ the weighted average of the standard deviation of returns of the individual securities.

A. less than
B. greater than
C. equal to
D. less than or equal to

29. Emily, age 68, purchased a variable annuity for $28,000. The annuity provides annual variable payments for life. If Emily's life expectancy is 14 years, the amount of each $3,000 annual payment that can be excluded from ordinary income is:

A. $0.
B. $1,000.
C. $2,000.
D. $3,000.

30. Which of the following is a contract entered into between two people before a marriage or civil union?

A. Separation agreement
B. Prenuptial agreement
C. Partnership agreement
D. Postnuptial agreement

31. Which of the following is a type of profit sharing plan in which elective salary deferrals are made with pre-tax dollars and are excluded from an employee's taxable income?

A. 401(k) plan
B. 529 plan
C. Pension plan
D. Defined benefit plan

32. For the ______ form of property ownership, when the owner dies, the property may be distributed according to the owner's will or through intestate succession.

A. tenancy by entirety
B. JTWROS
C. fee simple
D. cooperative

33. All but which of the following are examples of qualitative data?

A. Goals
B. Yields
C. Lifestyle
D. Priorities

34. Which of the following involves dividing an investment portfolio among different categories, such as stocks, bonds, and cash?

A. Fundamental analysis
B. Asset allocation
C. Sector rotation
D. Momentum investing

35. Jason wants to give his nephew $15,000 to take a trip around the world in 8 years. How much should he invest today at an annual rate of 5% compounded annually to have $15,000 in 8 years?

A. $10,152.59
B. $11,330.64
C. $13,913.55
D. $15,070.89

36. Which of the following is correct regarding the maturities of Treasury bills, Treasury notes, and Treasury bonds?

A. Treasury notes have maturities of 10 years or more.
B. Treasury bills have maturities of 1 year or more.
C. Treasury bonds have maturities greater than 10 years.
D. All of the above are correct.

37. Which of the following provides for the orderly administration of a decedent's estate and provides clean title to a decedent's property?

A. Advance directive
B. Living will
C. Codicil
D. Probate

38. Distributions from a 401(k) plan following separation from service after age ______ are not subject to the ______ premature distribution penalty.

A. 50; 10%
B. 50; 20%
C. 55; 10%
D. 55; 20%

39. All but which of the following are eligible tax filing statuses in the United States?

A. Single
B. Domestic partner
C. Married filing jointly
D. Married filing separately

40. Which of the following will result from selling an asset for less than its adjusted basis?

A. Capital loss
B. Capital gain
C. Offsetting loss
D. Offsetting gain

41. A ______ provides the decedent/grantor's estate with the unlimited marital deduction while, at the same time, ensuring the decedent retains control over the ultimate disposition of his or her property.

A. marital trust
B. credit shelter trust
C. QTIP trust
D. revocable trust

42. Which of the following is the risk that a bond's coupon payment will be used to purchase securities at a lower interest rate than the original yield?

A. Reinvestment risk
B. Purchasing power risk
C. Market risk
D. Default risk

43. All but which of the following are correct regarding nonqualified deferred compensation plans?

A. They can provide executives with customized retirement plans.
B. They are subject to qualified plan nondiscrimination rules.
C. They can provide retirement benefits in excess of qualified plan limits.
D. All of the above are correct.

44. In a ______ state, assets acquired by one member of a married couple are deemed to belong to that person, unless they were titled in both names.

A. community property
B. common law
C. tenancy in common
D. joint tenancy

45. Brian deposited $325 into a money market account at the end of each month for the past 3 years. His account is now valued at $12,875. If interest was compounded monthly, what was the average annual compound rate of return that Brian earned over the 3-year period?

A. 6.5%
B. 6.9%
C. 7.3%
D. 7.8%

46. A special catch up provision is permitted for employees with at least 15 years of service in which of the following plans?

A. 401(k) plan
B. 403(b) plan
C. 457 plan
D. All of the above are correct.

47. At what age do most individuals qualify for Medicare?

A. 55
B. 59
C. 60
D. 65

48. Which of the following is the appointed legal representative of a decedent whose responsibilities may include collecting assets of the deceased, paying creditors, and distributing remaining assets to heirs or other beneficiaries?

A. Estate trustor
B. Estate beneficiary
C. Estate administrator
D. Estate grantor

49. Which of the following is a type of professional liability insurance that is generally best suited for financial planners, insurance agents, and real estate brokers who can cause financial harm to another person?

A. Malpractice insurance
B. Errors and omissions insurance
C. Business overhead insurance
D. Commercial umbrella insurance

50. Mike, age 65, has made lifetime contributions of $25,000 into his Roth IRA. This account is now valued at $32,000. If Mike withdraws $4,000 to pay for a vacation, how much of the withdrawal is taxable?

A. $0
B. $3,000
C. $4,000
D. $7,000

51. All but which of the following are correct regarding the difference between a 15-year mortgage and a 30-year mortgage?

A. A 15-year mortgage will generally charge a higher interest rate.
B. A 15-year mortgage will have a higher monthly payment, but less interest will be paid overall.
C. Assuming no prepayment penalty, a 30-year mortgage can be repaid over 15 years if the borrower chooses to make extra payments.
D. All of the above are correct.

52. Which of the following is/are correct regarding COBRA continuation coverage?

(1) It is provided to employees who have changed from full-time to part-time status.
(2) It is provided to spouses and dependents of a covered employee due to the employee's death, divorce, legal separation, or eligibility for Medicare.

A. (1) only
B. (2) only
C. None of the above are correct.
D. All of the above are correct.

53. All but which of the following are correct regarding health insurance plans under the Affordable Care Act (ACA)?

A. Once an individual has enrolled in a Marketplace plan, he or she cannot be denied coverage or have premiums increased based only on health status.
B. Certain low-income individuals may qualify for government subsidies to help pay for health insurance costs.
C. Grandfathered health plans must cover pre-existing conditions and preventive care.
D. All of the above are correct.

For questions 54 – 56, match the disability policy renewal provision with the description that follows. Use only one answer per blank. Answers may be used more than once or not at all.

A. Guaranteed renewable
B. Cancellable
C. Conditionally renewable
D. Noncancellable

54. ____ The policy may not be canceled by the insurance company during the policy term, but the company may refuse to renew the policy for specific reasons listed in the contract.

55. ____ The premium schedule will never change unless the insured buys additional coverage in the future.

56. ____ The insured has the right to renew the policy for a stated number of years. Premiums cannot change unless the change is made for an entire class of policyholders.

57. All but which of the following are characteristics of mutual funds?

A. They provide professional management.
B. They provide diversification.
C. They have minimal transaction costs.
D. They trade throughout the day like stocks.

58. Which of the following is/are correct regarding investment risk in a qualified retirement plan?

(1) In a defined contribution plan, the employer bears the investment risk.
(2) In a defined benefit plan, the employee bears the investment risk.

A. (1) only
B. (2) only
C. None of the above are correct.
D. All of the above are correct.

59. Paraphrasing and summarizing are forms of ______ between an advisor and client.

A. directive counseling skills
B. nondirective counseling skills
C. emotional biases
D. cognitive errors

60. Which of the following is a binding agreement between co-owners of a business that defines the process for transferring an ownership interest if a co-owner dies, becomes disabled, or leaves the business?

A. Articles of incorporation
B. Buy-sell agreement
C. Postnuptial agreement
D. Modified endowment contract

61. Logan's annual gross income is $100,000. If he pays $25,000 in annual income tax, then his total housing debt costs, including principal, interest, taxes, and insurance, should not exceed ______ per month.

A. $1,166.67
B. $1,750.00
C. $2,333.33
D. $3,000.00

62. Which of the following is a second probate that may be required in addition to a decedent's primary probate?

A. Testamentary probate
B. Ancillary probate
C. Testate administration
D. Testate succession

63. Which of the following has low default risk, a low real return, and is easily converted to cash?

A. Mortgage-backed security
B. Corporate bond
C. Promissory note
D. Money market fund

64. The retirement plan known as a "SEP" is a:

A. Simplified Employee Pension.
B. Self Employed Plan.
C. Stock Equity Program.
D. Supplemental Employer Plan.

65. Which of the following is/are correct regarding a bond's coupon?

(1) The smaller a bond's coupon, the greater its relative price fluctuation.
(2) The smaller a bond's coupon, the greater its reinvestment risk.

A. (1) only
B. (2) only
C. None of the above are correct.
D. All of the above are correct.

66. Which of the following refers to the ability of an estate to pay fees and expenses without having to sell assets?

A. Estate solvency
B. Estate stability
C. Estate liquidity
D. Estate marketability

67. Which of the following is correct regarding a FICO score?

A. A higher FICO score indicates a lower default risk which results in a lower cost of borrowing.
B. A higher FICO score indicates a higher default risk which results in a higher cost of borrowing.
C. A higher FICO score indicates a lower default risk which results in a higher cost of borrowing.
D. A higher FICO score indicates a higher default risk which results in a lower cost of borrowing.

68. Which of the following provides an insurer with the legal right to seek reimbursement from the person or entity responsible for an accident after the insurer has paid the insured's claim?

A. Indemnification
B. Subrogation
C. Rescission
D. Coinsurance

69. Which of the following is/are correct regarding ERISA?

(1) ERISA requires plan sponsors to disclose full and accurate information about qualified retirement plan activity to all participants.
(2) ERISA provides mandatory insurance for defined benefit plans.

A. (1) only
B. (2) only
C. None of the above are correct.
D. All of the above are correct.

70. Which of the following is a type of emotional bias in behavioral finance that refers to an individual's tendency to make financial decisions that are familiar and comfortable even though pursuing change may be beneficial?

A. Affinity bias
B. Conservatism bias
C. Self-control bias
D. Status quo bias

71. Which of the following describes a Series I bond?

A. A savings bond that is sold at a deep discount from par value.
B. A savings bond that earns a variable rate of interest that is tied to the rate of inflation.
C. A savings bond that is guaranteed to double in value in 20 years.
D. A savings bond issued by local municipalities that pays monthly interest.

72. Which of the following is a savings plan used to pay for qualified education expenses at primary, secondary, and post-secondary institutions?

A. REMIC
B. ESOP
C. CESA
D. DRIP

73. On which of the following financial statements would an individual's remaining mortgage balance be provided?

A. Statement of financial position
B. Cash flow statement
C. Income statement
D. None of the above are correct.

74. All but which of the following are correct regarding a mutual fund's expense ratio?

A. It is usually expressed as a percentage rather than a flat dollar amount.
B. It represents the cost of operating a fund.
C. It is deducted from the fund's total value on a regular basis rather than being itemized on an investor's account statement.
D. Actively managed funds typically have lower expense ratios than passively managed funds.

75. All but which of the following are correct regarding the inheritance tax?

A. The tax is due when property is received from the estate of a deceased person.
B. Similar to the federal estate tax, the estate is responsible for paying the tax, not the beneficiary.
C. Not every state has an inheritance tax.
D. All of the above are correct.

ANSWER KEY

1. C
A zero-coupon bond is sold at a deep discount from face value and does not pay interest prior to maturity.

2. B
The major credit bureaus in the United States are Equifax, Experian, and TransUnion.

3. A
With a non-durable power of attorney, the agent's ability to act on behalf of the principal stops in the event of the principal's incapacity.

4. A
A life insurance policy that pays a dividend is a participating policy.

5. D
The FDIC provides deposit insurance to protect customer money in the event of a bank failure.

6. B
A mutual fund that invests only in securities outside the U.S. is an international fund.

7. B
Higher risk bonds have higher yields to maturity. If a bond's coupon rate is greater than its yield to maturity, the bond will sell at a premium.

8. A
A will is a legal document that coordinates the distribution of probate property after death and can appoint guardians for minor children.

9. D
To make an inter vivos gift, the donor must be legally competent; the donee must be capable of receiving and possessing the property; there must be delivery to, and acceptance by, the donee or the donee's agent; and the donor must make a "complete" gift.

10. B
Par value is the principal amount that an investor will be paid upon maturity of a bond.

11. A
A noncontributory pension plan is a type of retirement plan in which only the employer contributes money toward the retirement benefits of the employees. (It is "noncontributory" because employees are not permitted to contribute.)

12. D
A fiduciary under the provisions of ERISA is an individual that has discretionary authority or responsibility over plan administration, exercises discretionary authority over plan management, provides investment advice for a fee or other compensation, or exercises authority or control over the disposition of plan assets.

13. B
A load is a sales charge that may be imposed when an investor purchases mutual fund shares through an investment company.

14. A
When Dawn dies the 401(k) plan will pass to Rich because the beneficiary designation bypasses the will.

15. A
Unemployment compensation is included in income.

16. B
Military combat pay is excluded from income.

17. A
Prizes are included in income.

18. A
Tips and gratuities are included in income.

19. C
Flood is a common exclusion from a homeowners insurance policy.

20. D
Business risk is a type of unsystematic risk.

21. C
The maximum percentage of Social Security benefits that may be subject to tax is 85%.

22. B
Reinvesting an investment's earnings so that it produces additional gains over time is known as compounding.

23. D
Common stock is referred to as equity because the owner of the stock is also an owner of the corporation and may participate in its capital and income growth.

24. C
Adjusted basis = cost + expenses of sale – depreciation

25. B
There is no indication the client needs life insurance, and she will not be eligible to purchase disability insurance when she retires. Because the client is only 58 years old, she will need health insurance until she is eligible for Medicare at age 65. Even if she had COBRA continuation coverage, it would not last until age 65. Long-term care insurance is the best remaining answer of the choices provided.

26. B
A graduated payment mortgage is characterized by having payments that start small and increase over the life of the mortgage.

27. C
Within the Social Security system, AIME (average indexed monthly earnings) is used to calculate a worker's primary insurance amount.

28. D
If the securities in a portfolio are perfectly correlated, then the standard deviation of the portfolio will be equal to the weighted average of the standard deviations of the individual securities within the portfolio. If the securities in a portfolio are not perfectly correlated, then the standard deviation of the portfolio will be less than the weighted average of the standard deviations of the individual securities making up the portfolio. By adding more securities to a portfolio, the standard deviation of the portfolio can never increase.

29. C
Amount excluded from ordinary income = $28,000 / 14 years = $2,000

30. B
A prenuptial agreement is a contract entered into between two people before a marriage or civil union.

31. A
A 401(k) plan is a type of profit sharing plan in which elective salary deferrals are made with pre-tax dollars and are excluded from an employee's taxable income.

32. C
For the fee simple form of property ownership, when the owner dies, the property may be distributed according to the owner's will or through intestate succession.

33. B
Examples of qualitative data include goals, lifestyle, and priorities. Yields, such as the rate of return earned on fixed income investments, is an example of quantitative data.

34. B
Asset allocation involves dividing an investment portfolio among different categories, such as stocks, bonds, and cash.

35. A
FV = $15,000
n = 8
i = 5
PMT = 0
PV = ? = $10,152.59

36. C
Treasury bills have maturities of 1 year or less. Treasury notes have maturities of 10 years or less. Treasury bonds have maturities greater than 10 years.

37. D
Probate provides for the orderly administration of a decedent's estate and provides clean title to a decedent's property.

38. C
Distributions from a 401(k) plan following separation from service after age 55 are not subject to the 10% premature distribution penalty.

39. B
Eligible tax filing statuses in the United States include single, married filing jointly, and married filing separately.

40. A
Selling an asset for less than its adjusted basis will result in a capital loss.

41. C
A QTIP trust provides the decedent/grantor's estate with the unlimited marital deduction while, at the same time, ensuring the decedent retains control over the ultimate disposition of his or her property.

42. A
Reinvestment risk is the risk that a bond's coupon payment will be used to purchase securities at a lower interest rate than the original yield.

43. B
Nonqualified deferred compensation plans avoid qualified plan nondiscrimination rules and can provide retirement benefits in excess of qualified plan limits. Because of these features, they can provide executives with customized retirement plans.

44. B
In a common law state, assets acquired by one member of a married couple are deemed to belong to that person, unless they were titled in both names.

45. A
PMT = -$325
$n = 3 \times 12 = 36$
FV = $12,875
PV = 0
$i = ? = 0.5394 \times 12 = 6.5$

46. B
A special catch up provision is permitted for employees with at least 15 years of service in a 403(b) plan.

47. D
Most individuals qualify for Medicare at age 65.

48. C
An estate administrator is the appointed legal representative of a decedent whose responsibilities may include collecting assets of the deceased, paying creditors, and distributing remaining assets to heirs or other beneficiaries.

49. B
Errors and omissions insurance is a type of professional liability insurance that is generally best suited for financial planners, insurance agents, and real estate brokers who can cause financial harm to another person.

50. A
The withdrawal will not be taxable because it is a qualified distribution from a Roth IRA.

51. A
When comparing a 15-year mortgage and a 30-year mortgage, the 15-year mortgage will generally charge a lower interest rate and will have a higher monthly payment, but less interest will be paid overall. Assuming no prepayment penalty, a 30-year mortgage can be repaid over 15 years if the borrower chooses to make extra payments.

52. D
COBRA continuation coverage is provided to employees who have changed from full-time to part-time status. It is also provided to spouses and dependents of a covered employee due to the employee's death, divorce, legal separation, or eligibility for Medicare.

53. C
Grandfathered health plans are not required to cover pre-existing conditions or preventive care. Once an individual has enrolled in a Marketplace plan, he or she can't be denied coverage or have premiums increased based only on health status. Certain low-income individuals may qualify for government subsidies to help pay for health insurance costs.

54. C
A conditionally renewable policy may not be canceled by the insurance company during the policy term, but the company may refuse to renew the policy for specific reasons listed in the contract.

55. D
In a noncancellable policy, the premium schedule will never change unless the insured buys additional coverage in the future.

56. A
A guaranteed renewable policy gives the insured the right to renew the policy for a stated number of years. The insurer cannot change the premium unless the change is made for an entire class of policyholders.

57. D
Mutual funds have minimal transaction costs and provide professional management and diversification. Unlike stocks, mutual funds trade only once per day after the market closes.

58. C
In a defined contribution plan, the employee bears the investment risk. In a defined benefit plan, the employer bears the investment risk.

59. B
Paraphrasing and summarizing are forms of nondirective counseling skills between an advisor and client.

60. B
A buy-sell agreement is a binding agreement between co-owners of a business that defines the process for transferring an ownership interest if a co-owner dies, becomes disabled, or leaves the business.

61. C
Step 1: Maximum annual housing debt = $100,000 × 0.28 = $28,000
Step 2: Maximum monthly housing debt = $28,000 / 12 months = $2,333.33
Housing debt costs, including principal, interest, taxes, and insurance, should not exceed 28% of gross income.

62. B
Ancillary probate is a second probate that may be required in addition to a decedent's primary probate.

63. D
A money market fund has low default risk, a low real return, and is easily converted to cash.

64. A
The retirement plan known as a "SEP" is a Simplified Employee Pension.

65. A
The smaller a bond's coupon, the greater its relative price fluctuation, and the lower its reinvestment risk.

66. C
Estate liquidity refers to the ability of an estate to pay fees and expenses without having to sell assets.

67. A
A higher FICO score indicates a lower default risk which results in a lower cost of borrowing.

68. B
Subrogation provides an insurer with the legal right to seek reimbursement from the person or entity responsible for an accident after the insurer has paid the insured's claim.

69. A
ERISA requires plan sponsors to disclose full and accurate information about qualified retirement plan activity to all participants. The PBGC, not ERISA, provides mandatory insurance for defined benefit plans.

70. D
Status quo bias is a type of emotional bias in behavioral finance that refers to an individual's tendency to make financial decisions that are familiar and comfortable even though pursuing change may be beneficial.

71. B
A Series I bond is a savings bond that earns a variable rate of interest that is tied to the rate of inflation.

72. C
A CESA (Coverdell education savings account) is a savings plan used to pay for qualified education expenses at primary, secondary, and post-secondary institutions.

73. A
An individual's remaining mortgage balance would be provided on the statement of financial position.

74. D
A mutual fund's expense ratio represents the cost of operating a fund and is usually expressed as a percentage rather than a flat dollar amount. It is deducted from the fund's total value on a regular basis rather than being itemized on an investor's account statement. Actively managed funds typically have higher expense ratios than passively managed funds.

75. B
The inheritance tax is a state tax that is due when property is received from the estate of a deceased person. Unlike the federal estate tax, the beneficiary is responsible for paying the tax, not the estate. Not every state has an inheritance tax.

PRACTICE EXAM 12

QUESTIONS

1. Long-term care policies have which of the following characteristics?

A. Purchasing coverage is usually not necessary because Medicare will provide adequate protection.
B. Long-term care can be provided only in a hospital or skilled nursing care facility.
C. Benefits are triggered by cognitive impairment or the inability to perform activities of daily living (ADLs).
D. All of the above are correct.

2. To modify or amend a will, a testator must execute which of the following?

A. Endorsement
B. Rider
C. Codicil
D. Provision

3. All but which of the following could be considered primary sources of retirement income?

A. Social Security
B. Medicaid
C. Personal savings and investments
D. Individual retirement accounts

4. Which of the following is a form of bankruptcy that involves liquidating the majority of a debtor's assets and using the proceeds to pay creditors?

A. Chapter 7
B. Chapter 9
C. Chapter 11
D. Chapter 13

5. Which of the following is a written document that provides all material information about an offering of securities, and is the primary sales tool of the company that issues the securities?

A. Debenture
B. Proxy
C. Brochure
D. Prospectus

6. An improvement to a tangible asset has which of the following effects on the asset's basis?

A. The cost of the improvement is added to the asset's basis.
B. The cost of the improvement is subtracted from the asset's basis.
C. The cost of the improvement does not change the asset's basis.
D. None of the above are correct.

7. Which of the following is/are correct regarding a power of appointment?

(1) Only tangible property may be subject to a power of appointment.
(2) A power of appointment may be general or limited in nature.

A. (1) only
B. (2) only
C. None of the above are correct.
D. All of the above are correct.

8. Which of the following is the person or entity that has the exclusive authority and discretion to manage and control the assets of a qualified retirement plan?

A. Auditor
B. Trustee
C. Accountant
D. Executor

9. The "maximum out-of-pocket" (MOOP) is most closely associated with which of the following lines of insurance?

A. Umbrella insurance
B. Disability insurance
C. Health insurance
D. Homeowners insurance

10. Which of the following is an item of value that a lender can seize from a borrower upon failure to repay a loan?

A. Collateral
B. Corpus
C. Deposit
D. Principal

11. Which of the following is the risk that investors will not find a market for their securities, which may prevent them from buying or selling when they want?

A. Market risk
B. Liquidity risk
C. Finance risk
D. Regulatory risk

12. Which of the following plans require immediate vesting?

A. Employer contributions to a 401(k) plan.
B. Employer contributions to a SEP.
C. Employer contributions to a money purchase plan.
D. All of the above are correct.

13. In which of the following trusts is the surviving spouse given a general power of appointment by the decedent spouse to distribute the decedent's property as the surviving spouse determines? Since the surviving spouse holds a general power of appointment, he or she may use trust assets to benefit him or herself directly.

A. Marital trust
B. Credit shelter trust
C. QTIP trust
D. Estate trust

14. An investment advisor that is registered with either its state securities regulator or the SEC is a/an:

A. CLU.
B. CEP.
C. RIA.
D. RFP.

15. Ben is an employee of Gamma Corporation. As an employee, he does not have to report any income with respect to the first ______ of life insurance coverage provided by Gamma Corporation through a group plan.

A. $25,000
B. $50,000
C. $75,000
D. $100,000

16. All but which of the following are correct regarding health insurance plans under the Affordable Care Act (ACA)?

A. All Marketplace plans must cover 3 essential health benefits at a minimum.
B. All Marketplace plans must offer dental coverage for children, but dental benefits for adults are optional.
C. All Marketplace plans must cover treatment for pre-existing medical conditions.
D. All of the above are correct.

17. Which of the following is/are correct regarding the generation-skipping transfer tax (GSTT)?

(1) GSTT is imposed as a flat tax at the highest federal estate tax rate for the year of the transfer.
(2) GSTT is imposed instead of any gift and/or federal estate taxes that may apply.

A. (1) only
B. (2) only
C. None of the above are correct.
D. All of the above are correct.

18. Which of the following is a type of education tax credit?

A. Academic achievement credit
B. Lifetime learning credit
C. Education advancement credit
D. Continuing learning credit

19. All but which of the following are correct regarding blue chip stocks?

A. They generally provide a long-term hedge against inflation.
B. The Dow Jones Industrial Average consists of 30 blue chip stocks.
C. They have a history of not distributing dividends.
D. None of the above are correct.

20. Which of the following is a distribution or payment made within a single tax year of a retirement plan participant's entire account balance?

A. Deferred distribution
B. Serial distribution
C. Disability distribution
D. Lump sum distribution

21. In a/an ______ there is no legal distinction between the owner and the business.

A. S corporation
B. C corporation
C. sole proprietorship
D. LLC

22. Which of the following is a professionally managed investment company that invests in a diversified portfolio of real estate properties and mortgages?

A. SPAC
B. REIT
C. ADR
D. CDS

23. Tim, age 28, has a wife and two children. He earns a high income but manages to save very little. Unfortunately, Tim doesn't think this will ever change. He'd like to purchase a life insurance policy that will force him to save money. Which insurance policy is most suitable to meet Tim's goals?

A. Second-to-die whole life
B. 20-year term
C. Universal life
D. Whole life

24. An IRA must be created and funded by ______ of the calendar year following the year in which the contribution applies.

A. January 1st
B. April 15th
C. June 30th
D. December 31st

25. Which of the following Acts entitles consumers to one free credit report every 12 months from each of the three credit bureaus?

A. Truth in Lending Act (TILA)
B. Equal Credit Opportunity Act (ECOA)
C. Fair and Accurate Credit Transactions Act (FACTA)
D. Fair Credit Billing Act (FCBA)

26. All but which of the following are correct regarding capital losses?

A. Short-term capital losses may offset short-term capital gains.
B. Long-term capital losses may offset long-term capital gains.
C. Unused capital losses retain their original character as either short-term or long-term in nature.
D. All of the above are correct.

27. After a loss resulting from an automobile accident, the insured is expected to do which of the following?

(1) Permit the insurer to gather medical reports and other relevant records.
(2) Send the insurer notices and legal documents related to the claim.
(3) Submit proof of loss when required by the insurer.
(4) Submit to a physical exam at the insurer's request if it is relevant to the claim.

A. (1) and (3) only
B. (1), (2), and (3) only
C. (2), (3), and (4) only
D. All of the above are correct.

28. With the JTWROS form of property ownership, which of the following occurs when one owner dies?

A. The decedent's share is distributed to the surviving owners, and the property avoids probate.
B. The decedent's share is distributed to the surviving owners, and the property goes through probate.
C. The decedent's share is distributed according to the will, and the property goes through probate.
D. The decedent's share is distributed according to the will, and the property avoids probate.

29. Which of the following is the formula to calculate an individual's effective tax rate?

A. Effective tax rate = total tax paid / taxable income
B. Effective tax rate = taxable income / total tax paid
C. Effective tax rate = total tax paid × taxable income
D. None of the above are correct.

30. All but which of the following are types of systematic risk?

A. Purchasing power risk
B. Financial risk
C. Market risk
D. Exchange rate risk

31. In a/an ______ transfer, funds are moved from one retirement plan to another without the account holder physically receiving the funds. Instead, two institutions facilitate the transfer on behalf of the account holder.

A. indirect
B. nonqualified
C. trustee-to-trustee
D. brokered

32. Which of the following are the two main types of credit?

A. Equity and debt
B. Liquid and illiquid
C. Installment and revolving
D. Inflow and outflow

33. Which of the following measures the level of a mutual fund's trading activity?

A. P/E ratio
B. Sharpe ratio
C. Standard deviation
D. None of the above are correct.

34. A/an ______ trust is established as part of the decedent's last will and testament, and therefore must go through probate.

A. GSTT
B. inter vivos
C. testamentary
D. living

35. Which of the following is the amount of take-home pay that an employee receives after taxes and deductions have been taken out of a paycheck?

A. Gross income
B. Taxable income
C. Passive income
D. Net income

The following information relates to questions 36 – 37.

Keith purchased a whole life insurance policy several years ago. He has provided the following information related to the policy.

Face amount: $250,000
Cash value: $87,500
Paid-up additions: $75,000
Cash value of paid-up additions: $50,000
Annual premium: $4,300
Annual dividend: $1,900

36. What is the current surrender value of Keith's policy?

A. $112,500
B. $137,500
C. $162,500
D. $164,500

37. If Keith dies, a death benefit of ______ will be paid to his beneficiary.

A. $250,000
B. $262,500
C. $300,000
D. $325,000

38. Which of the following is correct regarding the impact that a high estimated investment return has on achieving a financial goal?

A. It will require allocating fewer dollars toward achieving the goal.
B. It will require allocating more dollars toward achieving the goal.
C. It will not affect the amount of dollars required to achieve the goal.
D. It will require the cost of the financial goal to also increase.

39. Which of the following is referred to as a tax-sheltered annuity (TSA) plan?

A. 401(k) plan
B. 403(b) plan
C. 457 plan
D. 529 plan

40. Which of the following is the federal agency that shares information about companies and investment professionals to help investors make informed decisions and sets and enforces the rules that govern the securities markets?

A. Securities and Exchange Commission
B. Federal Reserve
C. ERISA
D. FinCEN

41. The part of Medicare that pays for medical insurance is:

A. Part A.
B. Part B.
C. Part C.
D. Part D.

42. All but which of the following are types of tax credits?

A. Adoption credit
B. Child tax credit
C. Child and dependent care credit
D. Student loan interest credit

43. Which of the following is a type of permanent life insurance that has flexible premiums and a flexible death benefit?

A. AD&D life insurance
B. Participating life insurance
C. Universal life insurance
D. Variable life insurance

44. Which of the following rules requires Registered Investment Advisors to provide clients with Form ADV Part 2?

A. Supplement rule
B. Solicitor rule
C. Brochure rule
D. Prospectus rule

45. Employer contributions to a defined benefit plan generally use either the ______ cliff vesting or ______ graded vesting schedules.

A. 1-year; 2-year
B. 2-year; 5-year
C. 3-year; 4-year
D. 5-year; 7-year

46. Which of the following represents the parts of a mortgage payment known as "PITI"?

A. Principal, income, term, interest
B. Principal, interest, taxes, insurance
C. Payment, income, term, insurance
D. Payment, insurance, taxes, income

47. Which of the following is/are correct regarding survivorship life insurance?

(1) It is referred to as second-to-die life insurance.
(2) Two death benefits are paid over the life of the policy.

A. (1) only
B. (2) only
C. None of the above are correct.
D. All of the above are correct.

48. Which of the following is a form filed by a taxpayer to make corrections to a tax return from a previous year?

A. Excise return
B. Appealed return
C. Supplemental return
D. Amended return

49. Which of the following is a formal contract between a bond issuer and a bondholder that describes the terms and conditions of a bond?

A. Indenture agreement
B. Debenture agreement
C. Underwriting agreement
D. Rights offering

50. Which of the following is the amount of money that an insured must pay before the insurance policy begins paying for covered expenses?

A. Stop-loss
B. Indemnity
C. Deductible
D. Premium

51. All but which of the following are exempt from COBRA continuation coverage?

A. Government employers
B. Church employers
C. Employers with less than 20 employees
D. All of the above are correct.

52. Which of the following steps of the financial planning process comes directly after identifying and selecting goals?

A. Presenting the financial planning recommendations.
B. Developing the financial planning recommendations.
C. Analyzing the client's current course of action and potential alternate courses of action.
D. Understanding the client's personal and financial circumstances.

53. If comparable bonds are yielding 11.2%, what is the current price of a $1,000 face value bond that pays a 9% semiannual coupon payment and matures in 7 years?

A. $819.14
B. $840.88
C. $895.17
D. $908.04

54. All but which of the following are types of municipal bonds?

A. Credit bonds
B. General obligation bonds
C. Revenue bonds
D. Private activity bonds

55. Rich and Abby are married and live in a community property state. Which of the following is considered community property?

A. A car, acquired during marriage from a joint bank account, titled in Abby's name.
B. A boat, acquired before marriage from a joint bank account, titled in Rich's name.
C. Jewelry inherited by Abby during marriage, titled in her name.
D. Artwork inherited by Rich before marriage, titled in his name.

56. All but which of the following are types of IRAs?

A. Roth IRA
B. SIMPLE IRA
C. SEP IRA
D. Joint IRA

57. For disability insurance, a longer elimination period will result in a/an ______ premium.

A. adjustable
B. graduated
C. higher
D. lower

58. The two broad categories of defined contribution plans are:

A. qualified plans and nonqualified plans.
B. personal plans and employer plans.
C. profit sharing plans and pension plans.
D. defined benefit plans and pension plans.

59. Edward earns an annual income of $95,000, and he would like to purchase a new house. He expects to make a 20% down payment and finance the remaining amount. If the mortgage lender will provide a loan equal to 2.5 times annual income, what is the maximum house price that Edward can afford?

A. $190,000
B. $237,500
C. $284,425
D. $296,875

For questions 60 – 62, match the type of risk with the description that follows. Use only one answer per blank. Answers may be used more than once or not at all.

A. Business risk
B. Tax risk
C. Financial risk
D. Market risk
E. Credit risk
F. Country risk

60. ____ The risk associated with a company using debt as part of its capital structure.

61. ____ The possibility that a bond issuer will default.

62. ____ The risk inherent in company operations.

63. In a life estate, property ownership is split between which of the following?

A. A charitable interest and a remainder interest
B. A grantor interest and a charitable interest
C. A present interest and a remainder interest
D. A beneficiary interest and a future interest

64. All but which of the following are definitions of disability that are commonly found in disability income policies?

A. Own occupation
B. Dual occupation
C. Modified own occupation
D. Any occupation

65. Which of the following are considered forfeitures from a retirement plan?

A. The account balance that an employee loses if plan assets face credit default.
B. The account balance that an employee loses if retirement plan investments lose value.
C. The vested account balance that an employee loses when leaving the company.
D. The non-vested account balance that an employee loses when leaving the company.

66. Which of the following is a type of cognitive error in behavioral finance that occurs when an individual overestimates his or her ability to control or influence the outcome of an event?

A. Mental accounting
B. Money illusion
C. Illusion of control
D. Self-attribution bias

67. As bond interest rates _____, duration _____.

A. increase; increases
B. decrease; increases
C. decrease; decreases
D. increase; is unchanged

68. Which of the following is the most common type of reverse mortgage?

A. HUD
B. HECM
C. NMLS
D. GSE

69. All but which of the following are correct regarding unsystematic risk?

A. It includes such risks as tax risk and exchange rate risk.
B. An investor who owns five growth stocks can reduce unsystematic risk by adding value stocks to the portfolio.
C. It is the risk associated with a particular security or company.
D. All of the above are correct.

70. Brandon's only assets at the time of his death were a house and a checking account, both titled in his name. Which of the following is/are correct regarding probate?

(1) If Brandon died testate, his property is subject to probate.
(2) If Brandon died intestate, his property avoids probate.

A. (1) only
B. (2) only
C. None of the above are correct.
D. All of the above are correct.

71. Which of the following entities is subject to double taxation?

A. LLC
B. Partnership
C. S corporation
D. C corporation

72. A _______ advisor charges a fee for service and can also receive commissions.

A. commission
B. pro bono
C. fee-based
D. fee-only

73. The gift tax annual exclusion is permitted for:

A. present interest gifts only.
B. future interest gifts only.
C. present and future interest gifts.
D. any gift under $10,000.

74. Epsilon Corporation provides its retired employees with a pension equal to 2.5% of final-average earnings per year for up to 25 years of service. If Eric has worked for Epsilon Corporation for 29 years and had final-average earnings of $90,000, how much will his pension be if he retires when he reaches 30 years of service?

A. $22,500
B. $33,750
C. $56,250
D. $67,500

75. The debt security known as an "ETN" is an:

A. equity-traded note.
B. exchange-traded note.
C. education-Treasury note.
D. equity-taxable note.

ANSWER KEY

1. C
Long-term care benefits are triggered by cognitive impairment or the inability to perform activities of daily living (ADLs). Long-term care can be provided in a variety of settings. Medicare is not likely to provide adequate long-term care protection.

2. C
To modify or amend a will, a testator must execute a codicil.

3. B
Primary sources of retirement income include Social Security, personal savings and investments, and individual retirement accounts.

4. A
Chapter 7 bankruptcy involves liquidating the majority of a debtor's assets and using the proceeds to pay creditors.

5. D
A prospectus is a written document that provides all material information about an offering of securities and is the primary sales tool of the company that issues the securities.

6. A
The cost of an improvement to a tangible asset is added to the asset's basis.

7. B
Both tangible and intangible property may be subject to a power of appointment. A power of appointment may be general or limited in nature.

8. B
The person or entity that has the exclusive authority and discretion to manage and control the assets of a qualified retirement plan is the trustee.

9. C
The "maximum out-of-pocket" (MOOP) is most closely associated with health insurance.

10. A
Collateral is an item of value that a lender can seize from a borrower upon failure to repay a loan.

11. B
Liquidity risk is the risk that investors will not find a market for their securities, which may prevent them from buying or selling when they want.

12. B
Employer contributions to a SEP require immediate vesting. A 401(k) plan and money purchase plan may use alternate vesting schedules.

13. A
In a marital trust (A-trust), the surviving spouse is given a general power of appointment by the decedent spouse to distribute the decedent's property as the surviving spouse determines. Since the surviving spouse holds a general power of appointment, he or she may use trust assets to benefit him or herself directly.

14. C
An investment advisor that is registered with either its state securities regulator or the SEC is an RIA (Registered Investment Advisor).

15. B
An employee does not have to report any income with respect to the first $50,000 of life insurance coverage provided by an employer through a group plan.

16. A
All Marketplace plans under the Affordable Care Act (ACA) must cover 10 essential health benefits at a minimum, must offer dental coverage for children (dental benefits for adults are optional), and must cover treatment for pre-existing medical conditions.

17. A
GSTT is imposed as a flat tax at the highest federal estate tax rate for the year of the transfer and in addition to any gift and/or federal estate taxes that may apply.

18. B
The lifetime learning credit is a type of education tax credit.

19. C
Blue chip stocks have a history of regularly distributing dividends and generally provide a long-term hedge against inflation. The Dow Jones Industrial Average consists of 30 blue chip stocks.

20. D
A lump sum distribution is a distribution or payment made within a single tax year of a retirement plan participant's entire account balance.

21. C
In a sole proprietorship there is no legal distinction between the owner and the business.

22. B
A REIT (real estate investment trust) is a professionally managed investment company that invests in a diversified portfolio of real estate properties and mortgages.

23. D
A second-to-die whole life policy is typically purchased for estate liquidity or to fund a specific goal at the death of the second spouse. Neither of these objectives are stated in the question. With the universal life policy, Tim would not be forced to pay the annual premium. The question states that Tim would like to purchase a policy that forces him to save money. A whole life policy will force Tim to pay premiums, act as a forced savings plan, and last for his entire lifetime.

24. B
An IRA must be created and funded by April 15th of the calendar year following the year in which the contribution applies.

25. C
The Fair and Accurate Credit Transactions Act (FACTA) entitles consumers to one free credit report every 12 months from each of the three credit bureaus.

26. D
Short-term capital losses may offset short-term capital gains. Long-term capital losses may offset long-term capital gains. Unused capital losses retain their original character as either short-term or long-term in nature.

27. D
After a loss resulting from an automobile accident, the insured is expected to permit the insurer to gather medical reports and other relevant records, send the insurer notices and legal documents related to the claim, submit proof of loss when required by the insurer, and submit to a physical exam at the insurer's request if it is relevant to the claim.

28. A
With the JTWROS (joint tenants with rights of survivorship) form of property ownership, when one owner dies the decedent's share is distributed to the surviving owners, and the property avoids probate.

29. A
Effective tax rate = total tax paid / taxable income

30. B
Purchasing power risk, market risk, and exchange rate risk are types of systematic risk. Financial risk is a type of unsystematic risk.

31. C
In a trustee-to-trustee transfer, funds are moved from one retirement plan to another without the account holder physically receiving the funds. Instead, two institutions facilitate the transfer on behalf of the account holder.

32. C
The two main types of credit are installment and revolving.

33. D
The turnover rate measures the level of a mutual fund's trading activity.

34. C
A testamentary trust is established as part of the decedent's last will and testament, and therefore must go through probate.

35. D
Net income is the amount of take-home pay that an employee receives after taxes and deductions have been taken out of a paycheck.

36. B
Surrender value = \$87,500 + \$50,000 = \$137,500

37. D
Death benefit = \$250,000 + \$75,000 = \$325,000

38. A
A high estimated investment return will require allocating fewer dollars toward achieving the goal.

39. B
A 403(b) plan is referred to as a tax-sheltered annuity (TSA) plan.

40. A
The Securities and Exchange Commission (SEC) is the federal agency that shares information about companies and investment professionals to help investors make informed decisions and sets and enforces the rules that govern the securities markets.

41. B
The part of Medicare that pays for medical insurance is Part B.

42. D
Types of tax credits include the adoption credit, child tax credit, and the child and dependent care credit.

43. C
Universal life insurance is a type of permanent life insurance that has flexible premiums and a flexible death benefit.

44. C
The brochure rule requires Registered Investment Advisors to provide clients with Form ADV Part 2.

45. D
Employer contributions to a defined benefit plan generally use either the 5-year cliff vesting or 7-year graded vesting schedules.

46. B
"PITI" includes principal, interest, taxes, and insurance.

47. A
Survivorship life insurance is known as second-to-die life insurance. The policy pays a death benefit only at the death of the second insured.

48. D
An amended return is a form filed by a taxpayer to make corrections to a tax return from a previous year.

49. A
An indenture agreement is a formal contract between a bond issuer and a bondholder that describes the terms and conditions of a bond.

50. C
The deductible is the amount of money that an insured must pay before the insurance policy begins paying for covered expenses.

51. D
Government employers, church employers, and employers with less than 20 employees are exempt from COBRA continuation coverage.

52. C
After identifying and selecting goals, the next step of the financial planning process is analyzing the client's current course of action and potential alternate courses of action.

53. C
FV = $1,000
n = 7 × 2 = 14
i = 11.2 / 2 = 5.6
PMT = $1000 × 0.09 = $90, then $90 / 2 = $45
PV = ? = $895.17

54. A
Types of municipal bonds include general obligation bonds, revenue bonds, and private activity bonds.

55. A
A car, acquired during marriage from a joint bank account, titled in Abby's name, is considered community property.

56. D
Types of IRAs include Roth, SIMPLE, and SEP.

57. D
For disability insurance, a longer elimination period will result in a lower premium.

58. C
The two broad categories of defined contribution plans are profit sharing plans and pension plans.

59. D
Step 1: Maximum mortgage = $95,000 × 2.5 = $237,500
Step 2: Maximum purchase price = $237,500 / (1 – 0.2) = $296,875

60. C
Financial risk is the risk associated with a company using debt as part of its capital structure.

61. E
Credit risk is the possibility that a bond issuer will default.

62. A
Business risk is the risk inherent in company operations.

63. C
In a life estate, property ownership is split between a present interest and a remainder interest.

64. B
The definitions of disability that are commonly found in disability income policies are own occupation, modified own occupation, and any occupation.

65. D
The non-vested account balance that an employee forfeits when leaving the company are considered forfeitures from a retirement plan.

66. C
Illusion of control is a type of cognitive error in behavioral finance that occurs when an individual overestimates his or her ability to control or influence the outcome of an event.

67. B
As bond interest rates decrease, duration increases.

68. B
A HECM (home equity conversion mortgage) is the most common type of reverse mortgage.

69. A
Unsystematic risk is the risk associated with a particular security or company. Tax risk is an unsystematic risk, but exchange risk is a systematic risk. An investor who owns five growth stocks can reduce unsystematic risk by adding value stocks to the portfolio.

70. A
Brandon's property will be subject to probate whether he died testate or intestate since no will substitutes were used.

71. D
A C corporation is subject to double taxation. Earnings are taxed once at the entity level and again at the individual level once distributions have occurred.

72. C
A fee-based advisor charges a fee for service and can also receive commissions.

73. A
The gift tax annual exclusion is permitted for present interest gifts only.

74. C
Step 1: 25 years × 2.5% per year = 62.5%
Step 2: 62.5% × $90,000 = $56,250

75. B
The debt security known as an "ETN" is an exchange-traded note.

PRACTICE EXAM 13

QUESTIONS

1. If an insurer accepts an insured's premium payment after the grace period has expired, the insurer has _______ its right to cancel the policy.

A. subrogated
B. enforced
C. waived
D. indemnified

2. Which of the following is correct regarding qualified distributions from a Roth IRA? (Assume qualified distributions are those taken after age 59 ½ that have met the five-year holding period requirement.)

A. They are tax-free and penalty-free.
B. They are taxable and penalty-free.
C. They are tax-free and will incur a penalty.
D. They are taxable and will incur a penalty.

3. Alan is purchasing a boat for $10,500. He is financing the boat at 11% compounded monthly for 4 years. How much is Alan required to pay at the end of each month to finance the boat?

A. $264.25
B. $266.47
C. $268.91
D. $271.38

4. For COBRA continuation coverage, a terminating employee must pay the employer's share of insurance premiums, but the total cost may not exceed _______ of the overall cost of providing coverage to employees.

A. 50%
B. 100%
C. 102%
D. 112%

5. Which of the following health plans generally provides the most flexibility to an individual choosing a healthcare provider and does not require a referral to see a specialist?

A. Preferred provider organization (PPO)
B. Health maintenance organization (HMO)
C. Optimal Health Network (OHN)
D. Comprehensive Healthcare Alliance (CHA)

6. All but which of the following are types of contributions that can be made by an employer into an employee's retirement plan?

A. Matching contributions
B. Nonelective contributions
C. Charitable contributions
D. Discretionary contributions

7. Which of the following is the risk associated with a single occurrence (natural disaster, terrorist attack, etc.) having a negative effect on the value of a security?

A. Financial risk
B. Event risk
C. Regulatory risk
D. Market risk

8. Bond ratings are primarily used to assess which of the following?

A. The creditworthiness of the bond issuer.
B. The likelihood that a bond will be called by the issuer.
C. The par value of a bond.
D. None of the above are correct.

9. Which of the following are permitted distribution options from qualified retirement plans?

(1) Direct trustee-to-trustee transfer.
(2) Payment in the form of an annuity or other periodic payment option.
(3) Transfer funds to a spouse's qualified retirement plan.
(4) Rollover funds from one qualified retirement plan to another.

A. (1) and (3) only
B. (1), (2), and (4) only
C. (2), (3), and (4) only
D. All of the above are correct.

10. "Intestate" means which of the following?

A. Dying in a state other than the state of domicile.
B. Dying without any assets.
C. Dying without a legally valid will.
D. Dying with a legally valid will.

11. Which of the following is the tendency for high-risk individuals to purchase greater amounts of insurance coverage than low-risk individuals?

A. Selection bias
B. Premium inequality
C. Adverse selection
D. Risk variation

12. Which of the following allows an employee to choose to have a portion of her paycheck withheld before taxes and contributed to a retirement plan?

A. DCPP
B. CODA
C. PERA
D. GARP

13. Which of the following is the last step of the financial planning process?

A. Analyzing the client's current course of action and potential alternate courses of action.
B. Implementing the financial planning recommendations.
C. Monitoring progress and updating.
D. Presenting the financial planning recommendations.

14. All but which of the following are correct regarding systematic risk?

A. It is the risk associated with the entire market.
B. It can only be minimized but cannot be eliminated through diversification.
C. Types of systematic risk include financial risk, default risk, and political risk.
D. It is referred to as non-diversifiable risk.

15. Which of the following is/are correct regarding the amount of property that may be gifted between U.S. citizen spouses?

A. Property may be gifted between spouses up to the annual exclusion limit without incurring gift tax.
B. Property may be gifted between spouses up to double the annual exclusion limit without incurring gift tax.
C. Property may be gifted between spouses up to the lifetime exclusion limit without incurring gift tax.
D. There is no limit on the amount of property that may be gifted between spouses without incurring gift tax.

16. Which of the following refers to the transfer of a life insurance policy to another party?

A. Assignment
B. Rollover
C. Designate
D. Convert

17. Christina teaches piano lessons at the local community center as an independent contractor. All but which of the following taxes is Christina required to pay?

A. Income tax
B. Corporate tax
C. Medicare payroll tax
D. Social security payroll tax

18. Which of the following is a type of cognitive error in behavioral finance that occurs when individuals attribute their successes to internal factors but blame their failures on external factors?

A. Conservatism bias
B. Self-attribution bias
C. Affinity bias
D. Status quo bias

19. When calculating Social Security benefits, "PIA" is the:

A. primary insurance amount.
B. protected income amount.
C. pension income adjustment.
D. personal income average.

20. Meredith wants to accumulate $105,000 in 8.5 years to fund her child's college education. She expects to earn an annual rate of 12.5% compounded quarterly. How much does she need to invest today to achieve her goal?

A. $36,882.01
B. $37,543.98
C. $38,793.35
D. $39,181.69

21. For Series I bonds, the "I" stands for:

A. interest.
B. inflation.
C. investment.
D. income.

22. All but which of the following are included in a decedent's probate estate?

A. A tenancy in common interest.
B. Life insurance payable to a beneficiary who is deceased.
C. Property held as tenancy by entirety.
D. Property owned outright in the decedent's name.

23. All but which of the following are types of itemized deductions?

A. Property taxes
B. IRA contributions
C. Mortgage interest
D. Charitable contributions

24. Which of the following refers to the person or entity legally responsible for holding and administering the assets of a trust in the interest of the beneficiary?

A. Trustee
B. Grantor
C. Executor
D. Trustor

25. Distributions from a/an _______ are tax-free if used to pay for qualified medical expenses.

A. CESA
B. GIC
C. UTMA
D. FSA

26. Which of the following is a likely outcome for an individual that has a high level of credit card debt?

A. Increased credit score.
B. Increased savings rate.
C. Increased interest payments.
D. Increased net worth.

27. Which of the following forms is used by investment advisors to register with the SEC or state securities authorities?

A. Form CRS
B. Form U5
C. Form ADV
D. Registration prospectus

28. A variable life insurance policy has which of the following characteristics?

A. A minimum death benefit is guaranteed.
B. Premiums and death benefits are flexible.
C. There is no cash value accumulation.
D. The death benefit is linked to the performance of the S&P 500 only.

29. Which of the following is a type of beneficiary designation that gives the policyholder the right to change the beneficiary without restriction?

A. Contingent
B. Primary
C. Revocable
D. Irrevocable

The following information relates to questions 30 – 32.

Juan had several capital gains and losses for the current year. His long-term capital gains were $3,200, his long-term capital losses were $2,800, his short-term capital gains were $800, and his short-term capital losses were $3,500.

30. What is the amount of net long-term capital gains?

A. $0
B. $400
C. $700
D. $2,400

31. What is the amount of net short-term capital gains?

A. –$2,700
B. –$700
C. –$400
D. $0

32. What is the total calculated capital gain or capital loss?

A. $2,300 net short-term capital loss
B. $2,300 net short-term capital gain
C. $3,000 net short-term capital loss
D. $3,000 net short-term capital gain

33. Which of the following is correct regarding contributions to a profit sharing plan?

A. Annual employer contributions to a profit sharing plan are mandatory.
B. Annual employer contributions to a profit sharing plan are not mandatory but must be substantial and recurring.
C. Annual employer contributions to a profit sharing plan do not need to be substantial and recurring.
D. None of the above are correct.

34. Which of the following is/are correct regarding traditional IRAs?

(1) Contributions may be fully or partially deductible depending on the taxpayer's AGI and tax filing status.
(2) Contributions and investment earnings are taxable until distributed.

A. (1) only
B. (2) only
C. None of the above are correct.
D. All of the above are correct.

35. Which of the following are financial securities indexed to the rate of inflation?

A. CDs
B. REITs
C. ETFs
D. TIPS

36. Which of the following is a gift in which the donee has an immediate right to use, possess, and enjoy the property and income derived from the property?

A. Reversionary gift
B. Remainder gift
C. Present interest gift
D. None of the above are correct.

37. Which of the following is the risk that a company's cash flows will not be sufficient to pay operating expenses?

A. Business risk
B. Concentration risk
C. Tax risk
D. Regulatory risk

38. All but which of the following are personal financial statements?

A. Statement of financial position
B. Statement of retained earnings
C. Cash flow statement
D. Budget

39. Which of the following prevents a life insurance policy from lapsing by issuing a loan from the policy's cash value to pay the premium after the grace period expires?

A. Surrender value provision
B. Automatic premium loan provision
C. Guaranteed insurability provision
D. Waiver of premium provision

40. Which of the following correctly describes the relationship between the standard deviation of an investment and its risk?

A. Higher standard deviation results in more risk.
B. Higher standard deviation results in less risk.
C. There is an inverse relationship between standard deviation and risk.
D. Standard deviation and risk are not correlated.

41. Evan and Diana have a daughter, age 18, who is preparing to start college this year. Although Evan and Diana earn a high income, they do not have adequate college savings already set aside and will need additional money. However, due to their high income, they won't qualify for a needs-based program. Which of the following should they consider?

(1) American opportunity credit
(2) 529 Plan
(3) PLUS loan
(4) Subsidized Stafford student loan

A. (1) and (2) only
B. (1) and (4) only
C. (2) and (3) only
D. (2) and (4) only

42. All but which of the following will avoid ancillary probate?

A. Irrevocable trust
B. Testamentary trust
C. Revocable living trust
D. All of the above are correct.

43. All but which of the following are correct regarding the "married filing separately" tax filing status?

A. A taxpayer who is married and filing separately may face a higher tax rate and pay more tax compared to filing jointly.
B. A taxpayer who is married and filing separately may be automatically disqualified from several of the tax deductions and credits available to taxpayers who file jointly.
C. The married filing separately tax filing status may be appropriate for current spouses who are planning to divorce and don't want to be accountable for each other's tax liability.
D. A taxpayer who is married but does not want to file separately may instead use the "single" filing status.

44. A fixed income security is subject to which of the following risks?

(1) Exchange rate risk
(2) Purchasing power risk
(3) Default risk
(4) Liquidity risk
(5) Reinvestment risk

A. (1), (2), (3), and (4) only
B. (1), (2), (4), and (5) only
C. (2), (3), (4), and (5) only
D. All of the above are correct.

45. Which of the following is a debt obligation that represents claims to the cash flows from pools of mortgage loans, most commonly on residential property?

A. Credit default swap
B. Mortgage paper
C. Mortgage-backed security
D. Collateralized loan obligation

46. All but which of the following are characteristics of whole life insurance?

A. It has a lower initial premium than term life insurance.
B. It may allow for the accumulation of cash value.
C. The policy owner may be different than the insured.
D. All of the above are correct.

47. Which of the following refers to a bond that is sold for less than face value?

A. Par bond
B. Callable bond
C. Discount bond
D. Premium bond

48. Which of the following is correct regarding required minimum distributions from a traditional IRA?

A. They must begin the same year that an individual retires, regardless of age.
B. They must begin no later than the year after an individual retires, regardless of age.
C. They are calculated based on the total amount contributed to the account.
D. None of the above are correct.

49. Patrick's annual gross income is $80,000. If he pays $20,000 in annual income tax, then his total debt payments should not exceed ______ per month.

A. $1,866.67
B. $2,200.33
C. $2,400.00
D. $2,600.67

50. Which of the following is the amount due to a policyholder upon surrendering a life insurance policy?

A. Premium value
B. Transfer value
C. Cash value
D. Collateral value

51. A "step-up in basis" at death refers to which of the following?

A. The increase in the market value of an asset upon the death of the owner.
B. The adjustment of an asset's cost basis to its fair market value upon the death of the owner.
C. The increase in capital gain taxes owed by the beneficiary upon inheriting an asset.
D. The exemption of an appreciated asset from the estate tax calculation upon the death of the owner.

52. Which of the following is a type of investment fund that aggregates money from accredited investors and uses a variety of strategies, such as derivatives and options, to generate returns?

A. Hedge fund
B. Commodity fund
C. Exchange-traded fund
D. Venture capital fund

53. Which of the following is a primary role of FINRA?

A. To oversee the stability of the U.S. financial system.
B. To provide an exchange to buy and sell securities.
C. To set minimum standards for retirement plans.
D. To regulate the securities industry.

54. Raising capital through an "IPO" refers to which of the following?

A. International private offering
B. Initial public offering
C. Initial price offering
D. Investment portfolio offering

55. Which of the following is a characteristic of group life insurance?

A. Benefits are not payable until the insured reaches a specific age.
B. Coverage is individually underwritten.
C. Coverage is generally provided through an employer.
D. Premiums can be paid only by the insured.

56. Which of the following can act as a will substitute?

A. An advance medical directive
B. A durable power of attorney
C. A living trust
D. A living will

57. Which of the following is correct regarding qualified retirement plans?

A. Withdrawals before age 59 ½ are subject to a 10% penalty.
B. Contributions must be made with after-tax dollars.
C. Contributions are not deductible by the employer.
D. Withdrawals are not subject to income tax.

58. All but which of the following are adjustments typically made when calculating an individual's taxable income?

A. Subtracting qualified business expenses.
B. Adding back income earned from tax-exempt bonds.
C. Subtracting contributions made to retirement accounts.
D. Including income earned from passive activities.

59. Which of the following describes the difference between a will and a living will?

A. A will is legally binding, while a living will is not.
B. A will is revocable, while a living will is irrevocable.
C. A will cannot be changed, while a living will can be changed through a codicil.
D. A will addresses asset distribution, while a living will addresses medical treatment.

60. Which of the following is correct regarding negative amortization?

A. It is the process of paying off a loan faster than originally scheduled.
B. It is the process of decreasing a loan balance through regular payments over time.
C. It occurs when loan payments are insufficient to pay down accruing interest.
D. It is the practice of obtaining a new loan to pay off an existing loan.

61. If interest rates ______ following a bond issue, a sinking fund provision will allow the issuer to reduce the interest rate risk of its bonds as it replaces a portion of the existing debt with ______ bonds.

A. decline; higher yielding
B. rise; higher yielding
C. decline; lower yielding
D. rise; lower yielding

62. Which of the following clauses in a will designates who will assume guardianship of minor children if the testator dies?

A. Executor appointment clause
B. Residuary clause
C. Survivorship clause
D. None of the above are correct.

63. Which of the following describes asset allocation?

A. Investing a portfolio into a single asset class to increase returns.
B. Investing a portfolio into low-risk securities to minimize risk.
C. Investing a portfolio into various asset classes to manage risk and optimize returns.
D. Investing a fixed amount of money into an asset class at regular intervals, regardless of price.

64. All but which of the following methods could be used to reduce an individual's tax liability?

A. Gift assets to family members to reduce estate taxes.
B. Avoid investing in tax-exempt municipal bonds.
C. Donate to charitable organizations to qualify for a tax deduction.
D. All of the above are correct.

65. An UGMA account has which of the following features?

A. Contributions are tax-deductible.
b. Funds must be used for qualified education expenses.
C. There is no annual contribution limit.
D. Only parents and legal guardians may contribute.

66. Automobile insurance typically covers which of the following?

A. Routine maintenance and minor repairs needed on a vehicle.
B. Personal belongings stolen from a vehicle.
C. Damage caused to a vehicle by floods or earthquakes.
D. Medical expenses for injuries sustained by an insured driver.

67. Which of the following describes the role of an executor when administering a will?

A. To oversee the implementation of the decedent's wishes outlined in the will.
B. To make decisions regarding the distribution of the decedent's assets.
C. To review and approve the final terms of the decedent's will.
D. To represent the decedent in legal proceedings.

68. Which of the following is generally correct regarding a corporate bond?

A. It provides the potential for unlimited gains if held to maturity.
B. It provides a fixed rate of interest.
C. It provides an investor with an ownership interest in the company.
D. It allows the investor to have corporate voting rights.

69. Which of the following is a characteristic of a lifecycle fund?

A. It automatically adjusts its asset allocation based on a target date.
B. It invests in either equities or fixed income, but not both.
C. It maintains a static asset allocation over time.
D. It focuses on high risk, high return investments.

70. Which of the following methods can be used to calculate life insurance needs?

(1) Human life value method
(2) Needs analysis method

A. (1) only
B. (2) only
C. None of the above are correct.
D. All of the above are correct.

71. If an individual dies without a will, which of the following determines the distribution of his or her assets?

A. Portability statutes
B. Bequest statutes
C. Intestate succession statutes
D. Testamentary statutes

72. The primary purpose of an investment policy statement (IPS) is to:

A. analyze market trends and provide investment recommendations.
B. execute trades and track investment performance.
C. ensure compliance with securities laws and regulations.
D. outline an investor's financial goals, risk tolerance, and investment objectives.

73. Which of the following is correct regarding the purpose of ABLE accounts?

A. To offer needs-based grants and scholarships for higher education expenses.
B. To allow tax-free withdrawals for a first-time home purchase for low-income families.
C. To provide tax advantages for qualified disability-related expenses.
D. All of the above are correct.

74. Which of the following is correct regarding nonqualified retirement plans?

A. Withdrawals are generally tax-free if made after age 59 ½.
B. Employee contributions are not deductible, but earnings grow tax-deferred until withdrawn.
C. They are subject to discrimination testing and must meet specific eligibility criteria.
D. All of the above are correct.

75. Which of the following is a type of mortgage that requires the borrower to make non-principal payments for a specific period of time, followed by fully amortizing payments for the remainder of the loan term?

A. Fixed-rate mortgage
B. Interest-only mortgage
C. Jumbo mortgage
D. Reverse mortgage

ANSWER KEY

1. C
If an insurer accepts an insured's premium payment after the grace period has expired, the insurer has waived its right to cancel the policy.

2. A
Qualified distributions from a Roth IRA are tax-free and penalty-free.

3. D
PV = -$10,500
n = 4 × 12 = 48
i = 11 / 12 = 0.9167
FV = 0
PMT = ? = $271.38

4. C
For COBRA continuation coverage, a terminating employee must pay the employer's share of insurance premiums, but the total cost may not exceed 102% of the overall cost of providing coverage to employees.

5. A
A preferred provider organization (PPO) generally provides the most flexibility to an individual choosing a healthcare provider and does not require a referral to see a specialist.

6. C
Matching, nonelective, and discretionary are types of contributions that can be made by an employer into an employee's retirement plan.

7. B
Event risk is the risk associated with a single occurrence (natural disaster, terrorist attack, etc.) having a negative effect on the value of a security.

8. A
Bond ratings are primarily used to assess the creditworthiness of the bond issuer.

9. B
The permitted distribution options from qualified retirement plans are lump sum distributions, direct trustee-to-trustee transfers, payments in the form of an annuity or other periodic payment option, and rollover of funds from one qualified retirement plan to another.

10. C
"Intestate" means dying without a legally valid will.

11. C
Adverse selection is the tendency for high-risk individuals to purchase greater amounts of insurance coverage than low-risk individuals.

12. B
CODA (cash or deferred arrangement) allows an employee to choose to have a portion of her paycheck withheld before taxes and contributed to a retirement plan.

13. C
The last step of the financial planning process is monitoring progress and updating.

14. C
Systematic risk is the risk associated with the entire market. It is referred to as non-diversifiable risk because it can only be minimized but cannot be eliminated through diversification. Financial risk, default risk, and political risk are types of unsystematic risk.

15. D
There is no limit on the amount of property that may be gifted between U.S. citizen spouses without incurring gift tax.

16. A
Assignment refers to the transfer of a life insurance policy to another party.

17. B
Christina will have to pay individual income tax plus self-employment tax (Social Security and Medicare tax) on her independent contractor income.

18. B
Self-attribution bias is a type of cognitive error in behavioral finance that occurs when individuals attribute their successes to internal factors but blame their failures on external factors.

19. A
When calculating Social Security benefits, "PIA" is the primary insurance amount.

20. A
FV = $105,000
n = 8.5 × 4 = 34
i = 12.5 / 4 = 3.125
PMT = 0
PV = ? = $36,882.01

21. B
For Series I bonds, the "I" stands for inflation.

22. C
A tenancy in common interest, life insurance payable to a beneficiary who is deceased, and property owned outright in the decedent's name are included in the probate estate. Property held as tenancy by entirety is not subject to probate and is not included in the probate estate.

23. B
Types of itemized deductions include property taxes, mortgage interest, and charitable contributions.

24. A
The trustee is the person or entity legally responsible for holding and administering the assets of a trust in the interest of the beneficiary.

25. D
Distributions from an FSA (flexible spending account) are tax-free if used to pay for qualified medical expenses.

26. C
A high level of credit card debt will likely result in increased interest payments, and a decreased credit score, savings rate, and net worth.

27. C
Form ADV is used by investment advisors to register with the SEC or state securities authorities.

28. A
Variable life insurance policies have fixed premiums and provide a guaranteed minimum death benefit. The cash value is linked to the performance of underlying investments, which may include the S&P 500.

29. C
A revocable beneficiary designation gives the policyholder the right to change the beneficiary without restriction.

30. B
$3,200 – $2,800 = $400 net long-term capital gain

31. A
$3,500 – $800 = $2,700 net short-term capital loss

32. A
$2,700 – $400 = $2,300 net short-term capital loss

33. B
Annual contributions to a profit sharing plan are not mandatory but must be substantial and recurring.

34. A
Contributions to a traditional IRA may be fully or partially deductible depending on the taxpayer's AGI and tax filing status. Contributions and investment earnings grow tax-free until distributed.

35. D
TIPS (Treasury inflation-protected securities) are financial securities indexed to the rate of inflation.

36. C
A present interest gift is a gift in which the donee has an immediate right to use, possess, and enjoy the property and income derived from the property.

37. A
Business risk is the risk that a company's cash flows will not be sufficient to pay operating expenses.

38. B
Personal financial statements include the statement of financial position, cash flow statement, and budget. The statement of retained earnings is a business financial statement.

39. B
An automatic premium loan provision prevents a life insurance policy from lapsing by issuing a loan from the policy's cash value to pay the premium after the grace period expires.

40. A
A higher standard deviation for an investment will result in more risk.

41. C
The 529 plan and PLUS loan are not based on financial need. The American opportunity credit and subsidized Stafford student loan are highly based on financial need, and Evan and Diana's child will likely not qualify.

42. B
A testamentary trust does not avoid probate because it is created by the will. Therefore, any property passing through a testamentary trust must first pass through probate.

43. D
A taxpayer who is married and filing separately may face a higher tax rate and pay more tax compared to filing jointly. The taxpayer may also be automatically disqualified from several of the tax deductions and credits available to taxpayers who file jointly. The married filing separately tax filing status may be appropriate for current spouses who are planning to divorce and don't want to be accountable for each other's tax liability. A taxpayer who is married cannot use the "single" filing status.

44. D
A fixed income security may be subject to all the risks listed. This includes systematic risks that are always present (exchange rate risk, purchasing power risk, reinvestment risk), as well as non-systematic risks such as default risk and liquidity risk.

45. C
A mortgage-backed security is a debt obligation that represents claims to the cash flows from pools of mortgage loans, most commonly on residential property.

46. A
Whole life insurance has a higher initial premium than term life insurance. Whole life policies may allow for the accumulation of cash value, and the policy owner may be different than the insured.

47. C
A bond that is sold for less than face value is a discount bond.

48. D
Required minimum distributions are calculated based on account value, not the amount contributed. The beginning date for required distributions is based on age, not the year of retirement.

49. C
Step 1: Maximum annual total debt = $80,000 × 0.36 = $28,800
Step 2: Maximum monthly total debt = $28,800 / 12 months = $2,400
Total debt payments should not exceed 36% of gross income.

50. C
The amount due to a policyholder upon surrendering a life insurance policy is the cash value.

51. B
A "step-up in basis" at death is the adjustment of an asset's cost basis to its fair market value upon the death of the owner.

52. A
A hedge fund is a type of investment fund that aggregates money from accredited investors and uses a variety of strategies, such as derivatives and options, to generate returns.

53. D
A primary role of FINRA is to regulate the securities industry.

54. B
Raising capital through an "IPO" refers to an initial public offering.

55. C
Group life insurance coverage is generally provided through an employer.

56. C
A living trust can act as a will substitute.

57. A
Withdrawals from qualified retirement plans before age 59 ½ are subject to a 10% penalty as well as income tax.

58. B
Adjustments typically made when calculating an individual's taxable income include subtracting qualified business expenses, subtracting contributions made to retirement accounts, and including income earned from passive activities.

59. D
A will addresses asset distribution, while a living will addresses medical treatment.

60. C
Negative amortization occurs when loan payments are insufficient to pay down accruing interest. This results in the principal balance increasing.

61. C
If interest rates decline following a bond issue, a sinking fund provision will allow the issuer to reduce the interest rate risk of its bonds as it replaces a portion of the existing debt with lower yielding bonds.

62. D
The "guardian clause" or "appointment of guardian clause" in a will designates who will assume guardianship of minor children if the testator dies.

63. C
Asset allocation refers to investing a portfolio into various asset classes to manage risk and optimize returns.

64. B
Methods that could be used to reduce an individual's tax liability include gifting assets to family members to reduce estate taxes and donating to charitable organizations to qualify for a tax deduction.

65. C
An UGMA account has no annual contribution limit.

66. D
Automobile insurance typically covers medical expenses for injuries sustained by an insured driver.

67. A
The role of an executor when administering a will is to oversee the implementation of the decedent's wishes outlined in the will.

68. B
A corporate bond provides a fixed rate of interest.

69. A
A lifecycle fund automatically adjusts its asset allocation based on a target date.

70. D
The human life value method and needs analysis method can be used to calculate life insurance needs.

71. C
If an individual dies without a will, intestate succession statutes determine the distribution of his or her assets.

72. D
The primary purpose of an investment policy statement (IPS) is to outline an investor's financial goals, risk tolerance, and investment objectives.

73. C
The purpose of ABLE accounts is to provide tax advantages for qualified disability-related expenses.

74. B

Employee contributions to nonqualified retirement plans are not deductible, but earnings grow tax-deferred until withdrawn.

75. B

An interest-only mortgage requires the borrower to make non-principal (interest only) payments for a specific period of time, followed by fully amortizing payments for the remainder of the loan term.

TIME VALUE OF MONEY

QUESTIONS

1. Liz has been investing $2,000 at the end of each year for the past 11 years. How much has she accumulated, assuming she has earned 8% compounded annually on her investments?

   A. $31,228.90
   B. $33,290.97
   C. $35,954.25
   D. $37,840.32

2. Pete purchased an investment for $750. He kept the investment for 6 years before selling it. If the internal rate of return for the 6-year period was 7%, what was the final selling price?

   A. $1,125.55
   B. $1,137.70
   C. $1,148.91
   D. $1,156.65

3. Jen wants to deposit an amount today that will last for 5 years. She needs to withdraw $1,300 at the beginning of each 6-month period, and she'll earn 8% compounded semi-annually on her investments. How much does she need to deposit to achieve her goal?

   A. $8,250.17
   B. $9,364.01
   C. $10,965.93
   D. $11,374.26

4. Arnold would like to save $80,000 for his son's college education. His son will begin college in 13 years. Assume Arnold can invest $10,000 now, and $600 at the end of each 3-month period. What annual rate of return is required for Arnold to achieve his goal?

   A. 1.90%
   B. 1.93%
   C. 7.59%
   D. 7.73%

5. Jane expects to receive $1,250,000 from a trust in 17 years. If the trust is earning an annual rate of 9% compounded quarterly, its current value is:

   A. $275,298.90.
   B. $277,346.01.
   C. $280,321.32.
   D. $283,902.87.

6. Leah purchased artwork for $30,000. She expects it will increase in value at a rate of 12% compounded annually for the next 4 years. How much will her artwork be worth at the end of the fourth year if her expectations are correct?

A. $37,212.44
B. $41,310.98
C. $47,205.58
D. $55,210.12

7. Carl invested $6,000 today with the promise that he will receive $11,000 in 4 years. If interest is compounded weekly, what is the average annual rate of return he will earn?

A. 9.48%
B. 12.72%
C. 13.99%
D. 15.18%

8. What is the current price of a zero-coupon bond with a $1,000 face value, a yield to maturity of 8.46%, and 5 years until maturity?

A. $620.47
B. $640.18
C. $660.80
D. $680.28

9. Louise invests $4,000 into her IRA. Each year, for the next 10 years, she is able to invest an additional $2,000. What will be the value of Louise's account at the end of 10 years if her investments earn 8% annually?

A. $20,337.42
B. $22,655.27
C. $37,608.82
D. $39,926.67

10. Lauren expects to receive $150,000 from a pension in 7 years. What is the current value of the pension if it is earning an annual rate of 10% compounded quarterly?

A. $75,131.67
B. $76,274.38
C. $83,485.10
D. $84,273.10

11. Jack has been investing $3,200 at the end of each 6-month period to accumulate funds for his daughter's college tuition. The funds are earning an annual rate of 5% compounded semiannually. When Jack's daughter begins college in 6 years, how much will the account be worth?

A. $40,763.45
B. $42,526.78
C. $43,992.15
D. $44,145.77

12. Paula invests $4,000 today with the expectation that she will receive $9,000 in 5 years. If interest is compounded weekly, what is the average annual rate of return that Paula will earn?

A. 13.38%
B. 14.12%
C. 15.85%
D. 16.24%

13. What is the current market price of a bond that pays a 10% coupon and matures in 8 years? Comparable bonds are yielding 12.6%.

A. $489.04
B. $710.18
C. $871.29
D. $999.99

14. Jim wants to save $65,000 for a down payment on an apartment in 4 years. He can invest $1,200 at the beginning of each month, and he expects to earn 8% compounded monthly on his investments. How much will Jim have saved in 4 years?

A. $66,454.35
B. $68,070.70
C. $70,129.34
D. $72,310.18

15. Ryan would like to save $60,000 for his son's college education. His son will begin college in 12 years. Assume that Ryan can invest $15,000 now, and $500 at the end of each 3-month period. What annual rate of return is required for Ryan to achieve his goal?

A. 4.52%
B. 4.79%
C. 4.86%
D. 5.03%

16. Jessica wants to save $40,000 to purchase a vehicle in 3 years. She can invest $1,000 at the beginning of each month, and she expects to earn 10% compounded monthly on her investments. How much will Jessica have saved in 3 years? Will Jessica be able to achieve her goal?

    A. $40,278.48, No
    B. $41,781.57, No
    C. $42,130.00, Yes
    D. $43,182.37, Yes

17. Sam has a balloon payment of $50,000 due in 6 years. If he can make a lump sum payment today, how much should he offer to satisfy the loan if it is discounted at a rate of 8% compounded semiannually?

    A. $31,229.85
    B. $32,029.49
    C. $33,398.30
    D. $34,640.38

18. Michelle purchased a new condo for $160,000. She financed the condo at 6.5% compounded monthly for 30 years. What payment is Michelle required to make at the end of each month?

    A. $1,001.63
    B. $1,008.29
    C. $1,011.31
    D. $1,086.28

19. Carrie has been investing $4,125 at the end of each year for the past 18 years. Assuming that she has earned 6.35% compounded annually on her investments, she has accumulated a total of:

    A. $128,482.90.
    B. $131,794.07.
    C. $134,638.44.
    D. $137,120.73.

20. Melissa wants to accumulate $95,000 in 7.5 years to purchase a boat. She expects to earn an annual rate of 9.5% compounded quarterly. How much does Melissa need to invest today to achieve her goal?

    A. $46,979.26
    B. $48,292.38
    C. $49,840.25
    D. $50,283.49

21. Nick purchased an investment for $41,210. He expects it will increase in value at a rate of 7.25% compounded annually for the next 5 years. If his expectations are correct, how much will his investment be worth at the end of the fifth year?

A. $51,365.62
B. $54,599.34
C. $55,182.29
D. $58,477.54

22. Renee's bond has a market price of $910. The bond pays an 11% coupon and will mature in 6 years. What is the bond's yield to maturity?

A. 13.22%
B. 14.59%
C. 15.27%
D. 16.12%

23. Tracy wants to deposit an amount today that will last for 6 years. She needs to withdraw $1,400 at the beginning of each 6-month period and expects to earn 12% compounded semiannually on her investments. How much does Tracy need to deposit today to achieve her goal?

A. $10,673.59
B. $11,737.38
C. $12,441.62
D. $13,889.23

24. Jeff invested $10,000 in a high-yield account earning a 7% annual rate of return compounded monthly. What will be the value of Jeff's account at the end of 9 years?

A. $15,301.43
B. $16,692.90
C. $17,389.48
D. $18,741.77

25. Jon sued his former business partner and won a judgment that provides him $3,000 at the end of each 6-month period for the next 7 years. If the account that holds his settlement earns an average annual rate of 5% compounded semiannually, how much was the former partner initially required to pay Jon?

A. $33,170.16
B. $35,072.74
C. $37,517.24
D. $39,839.07

ANSWER KEY

1. B
PMT = –$2,000
n = 11
i = 8
PV = 0
FV = ? = $33,290.97

2. A
PV = –$750
n = 6
i = 7
PMT = 0
FV = ? = $1,125.55

3. C
Begin Mode
PMT = $1,300
n = 5 × 2 = 10
i = 8 / 2 = 4
FV = 0
PV = ? = $10,965.93

4. D
PV = –$10,000
n = 13 × 4 = 52
PMT = –$600
FV = $80,000
i = ? = 1.9322 × 4 = 7.73

5. A
FV = $1,250,000
n = 17 × 4 = 68
i = 9 / 4 = 2.25
PMT = 0
PV = ? = $275,298.90

6. C
PV = –$30,000
n = 4
i = 12
PMT = 0
FV = ? = $47,205.58

7. D
PV = –$6,000
n = 4 × 52 = 208
FV = $11,000
PMT = 0
i = ? = 0.2918 × 52 = 15.18

8. C
FV = \$1,000
n = 5 × 2 = 10
i = 8.46 / 2 = 4.23
PMT = 0
PV = ? = \$660.80

9. C
PV = –\$4,000
n = 10
i = 8
PMT = –\$2,000
FV = ? = \$37,608.82

10. A
FV = \$150,000
n = 7 × 4 = 28
i = 10 / 4 = 2.5
PMT = 0
PV = ? = \$75,131.67

11. D
PMT = –\$3,200
n = 6 × 2 = 12
i = 5 / 2 = 2.5
PV = 0
FV = ? = \$44,145.77

12. D
PV = –\$4,000
n = 5 × 52 = 260
FV = \$9,000
PMT = 0
i = ? = 0.3124 × 52 = 16.24

13. C
FV = \$1,000
n = 8 × 2 = 16
i = 12.6 / 2 = 6.3
PMT = \$1000 × 0.10 = \$100, then \$100 / 2 = \$50
PV = ? = \$871.29

14. B
Begin Mode
PMT = –\$1,200
n = 4 × 12 = 48
i = 8 / 12 = 0.6667
PV = 0
FV = ? = \$68,070.70

15. D
PV = -$15,000
n = 12 × 4 = 48
PMT = -$500
FV = $60,000
i = ? = 1.2573 × 4 = 5.03

16. C
Begin Mode
PMT = -$1,000
n = 3 × 12 = 36
i = 10 / 12 = 0.8333
PV = 0
FV = ? = $42,130.00
Yes, Jessica can achieve her goal because she will have more than $40,000.

17. A
FV = -$50,000
n = 6 × 2 = 12
i = 8 / 2 = 4
PMT = 0
PV = ? = $31,229.85

18. C
PV = -$160,000
n = 30 × 12 = 360
i = 6.5 / 12 = 0.5417
FV = 0
PMT = ? = $1,011.31

19. B
PMT = -$4,125
n = 18
i = 6.35
PV = 0
FV = ? = $131,794.07

20. A
FV = $95,000
n = 7.5 × 4 = 30
i = 9.5 / 4 = 2.375
PMT = 0
PV = ? = $46,979.26

21. D
PV = -$41,210
n = 5
i = 7.25
PMT = 0
FV = ? = $58,477.54

22. A
PV = –$910
n = 6 × 2 = 12
PMT = $1,000 × 0.11 = $110, then $110 / 2 = $55
FV = $1,000
i = ? = 6.6097 × 2 = 13.22

23. C
Begin Mode
PMT = $1,400
n = 6 × 2 = 12
i = 12 / 2 = 6
FV = 0
PV = ? = $12,441.62

24. D
PV = –$10,000
n = 9 × 12 = 108
i = 7 / 12 = 0.5833
PMT = 0
FV = ? = $18,741.77

25. B
PMT = –$3,000
n = 7 × 2 = 14
i = 5 / 2 = 2.5
FV = 0
PV = ? = $35,072.74

INDEX

A

B

C

L

M

N

Q

R

S

T

U

V

W - Z

Made in United States
Orlando, FL
29 June 2025

62469464R00184